Prague

- A ☛ in the text denotes a highly recommended sight
- A complete A–Z of practical information starts on p.103
- Extensive mapping on cover flaps

Berlitz Publishing Company, Inc.

Princeton Mexico City Dublin Eschborn Singapore

Berlitz Trademark Reg. U.S. Patent Office and other countries
Marca Registrada

Original text:	Ken Bernstein
Additional text:	Jaromír Douda, Brigitte Lee
Photography:	Chris Coe
Layout:	Media Content Marketing, Inc.
Cartography:	Falk-Verlag, Munich; Hard Lines

Although the publisher tries to insure the accuracy of all the information in this book, changes are inevitable and errors may result. The publisher cannot be responsible for any resulting loss, inconvenience, or injury. If you find an error in this guide, please let the editors know by writing to Berlitz Publishing Company, 400 Alexander Park, Princeton, NJ 08540-6306.

ISBN 2-8315-6317-8

Revised 1998 – Third Printing April 1999

Printed in Italy by Eurolitho S.r.l.

039/904 RP

Prague

PRAGUE AND ITS PEOPLE

For over a thousand years the architects of Prague have used every artifice ever invented to embellish their buildings, from Gothic arcades to Renaissance windows, on to Rococo angels and Art Nouveau sylphs. The locals simply take the resulting spectacle in their own stride, but Prague's unparalleled display of beautiful architectural history may just bowl you over.

Long before the "city of a hundred spires" had acquired its uplifting skyline, the setting itself was inspiring, with the wide, translucent Vltava River thrusting through the ancient settlement, with forested hills on every horizon. It all began to develop in the 14th century under a great king, who made history not only as the local potentate but as a ruler of the Holy Roman Empire.

Charles IV, a very cultivated monarch, gave orders for a glorious urban development programme, including a bridge that became more than just a way to get to the other side of the river. For five centuries it was Prague's only span across the Vltava. Today there are bridges up and down the river, but the Charles Bridge is still in use, and still indispensable. It will probably be the prettiest bridge you'll ever walk across, or happily linger upon.

Prague's rich heritage draws crowds of painters, photographers, and architecture students as well as ordinary tourists who, despite all they've heard and read, never fail to be astonished by the beauty of the place. Prague is even better than its publicity. Every detail—every tower and turret, pillar and portal—excels.

This architectural splendour might all have been destroyed in Europe's recent wars, but while World War II bombing raids ruined the historic hearts of many other Central European cities, Prague was largely spared. When the dust had settled, the Czech government invested a fortune in renovation. The avid conservation programme they began continues unabated today.

Prague, however, offers far more than expensively maintained castles and art relics. As a city of around 1.2 million people, it is a political, commercial, and, above all, thriving cultural capital that lives and breathes and enjoys itself.

Take the pulse of Prague at the crossroads of the modern city, Wenceslas Square, named after Prince Wenceslas I, who reigned here a thousand years ago. (The Christmas carol which upgraded him to "Good King Wenceslas" is a fanciful

The Karluv Bridge offers this lovely view of Prague Castle and Lesser Prague.

19th-century postscript.) Mix in with the crowd; you will see well-dressed women window-shopping, briefcase-burdened bureaucrats, proud parents all pushing their regal prams, and hordes of tourist groups chattering away to each other in countless languages. Queueing for an ice-cream cone will be a pleasant experience. The patient people of Prague never shove or argue while they wait; they have nothing to learn from the English when it comes to disciplined queueing.

Equipped with traditional manners, young people will still give up their bus seats to the elderly. The young generation is taller, better looking, and better dressed than ever before. A very few will go on to be film stars or tennis stars, but thousands will go on to university. Prague has a dozen institutions of higher learning (Einstein used to teach here). Charles University was founded in 1348, almost a century after the University College in Oxford, England, which makes it the oldest university in Central Europe.

You will soon get your bearings in Prague. The ancient Prague Castle complex still dominates the skyline, with the tranquil Lesser Quarter in its shadow. The fortified castle, once the seat of the kings of Bohemia, still rules; it's the headquarters of the president of the Czech Republic as well as an engrossing tourist attraction. Cross the bridge to the Gothic, Renaissance, and Baroque landmarks of the Old Town, and nearby, just six centuries old, the New Town.

On the way from castle to museum via historic church, stop at an outdoor café and watch the scene unfold. Perhaps try a traditional beer cellar or wine bar, so much a part of the capital's character. The Good Soldier Švejk, the most supreme malingerer of World War I, was the greatest advertisement for Prague taverns. In his triumph of passive resistance, the likeable Švejk had managed to bamboozle every official who had ever persecuted him. His Rabelaisian saga of the "little man" muddling through has inspired generations of Czechs. Like his creator, Jaroslav Hašek, Švejk tended to spend his evenings in the city's congenial taverns.

If you had to point to Prague (*Praha* in Czech) on a map of Europe you might well miss it, for it's farther north and west than most people imagine. The city is even more northerly than Canada's Winnipeg, although the climate is milder, and farther west than Vienna.

In the heart of Central Europe, on the political borderline between east and west, Prague is only around 312 km (193 miles) by motorway from Vienna and about 347 km (215 miles) from Berlin.

The city's area is a generous 497 km (192 square miles), about two-thirds the size of the vastly more populous New York City. This leaves plenty of space for Prague's extensive parks, forests, sports grounds, and zoo.

Central Prague, though, is as congested with cars as any other big city center. Road space is restricted by the priorities of pedestrian zones, and construction or reconstruction projects and new buildings are going up in all the suburbs—endless housing projects to ease the shortage of apartments.

Notwithstanding its rather westerly location on the map, 20th-century history assigned Prague to the eastern bloc for more than four decades. The red flags and proletarian slogans were

Street musicians on a corner at Prague Castle entertain passers-by.

swept away by the "velvet revolution" of 1989, when an upsurge of peaceful popular protest brought down the communist government.

Stalin's many statues may have been toppled, but other achievements still linger: highways, high-rises, and sports facilities. The most admirable of these is the city's clean and efficient Metro, the famous underground rail service that almost any city in the world could envy. At the last price report, a ticket was said to cost perhaps one-tenth of what it would in the west.

If getting around is cheap, fast, and easy, that's no reason to rush. This is a walking city, where every corner you may turn can reveal a new delight. Some of Prague's most memorable features can only be appreciated from close up: a street-corner shrine, a proudly sagging roof, a stately lamp post, a Cubist window.

Sightseeing out of the city, through picturesque orchards, verdant forests, and fragrant fields of hops, the order of the day is castles. In the Czech Republic, a country of 1,800 castles, the highlights are these fortified retreats of the old nobility, perched in commanding locations. Organized day trips from Prague can give you a choice of half a dozen important castles, each one offering something different. Closest is 14th-century Karlštejn, which was once reinforced by the Habsburgs; Konopiště, a Gothic castle transformed into a hunting lodge, is filled with the hunting trophies of Archduke Franz Ferdinand.

Another popular excursion features the spa of Karlovy Vary (or Karlsbad, as it was known to Bach, Goethe, and Peter the Great — see page 71), with a stop on the way at the tragically evocative village of Lidice (see page 77).

After a spate of sightseeing, Prague offers many forms of relaxation. The theatre is festive and, provided you buy tickets at the box office, very cheap. See Shakespeare in Czech,

A succession of bridges, old and new, span the city's ancient lifeline, the Vltava.

or the famous *Laterna Magika* multi-media spectacle. Music has always flourished here, whether it be a concert given by the Czech Philharmonic Orchestra, the grand opera, or a contemporary work. (Prague is where *Don Giovanni* had its premiere, Beethoven and Liszt performed, and the composers Smetana, Dvořák, and Janáček made their names.)

Alternatively, dine to the accompaniment of live music; forget *nouvelle cuisine* and dig into roast pork with cabbage immersed in a gravy that's substantial enough to float the dumplings. This culinary delight, which comes in bread or potato variants, is all but inevitable in Prague. Afterwards, you might wind up at a noisy nightclub, a boisterous cabaret, or even relaxing with a soothing drink in a quiet bar.

A BRIEF HISTORY

The long, often violent history of Prague reads like the wildly fluctuating fever chart of a hospital patient. In some eras Prague's suffering has been deep and long, but in others the city has been truly great.

Figures as distinguished as Good King Wenceslas, Holy Roman Emperor Charles IV, Jan Hus, and the Habsburg family fade in and out of the often lurid narrative, which flows as vividly as the blood spilled throughout the city's turbulent history.

For thousands of years travellers had been interested in the site of Prague, for it is a natural fording place on the Vltava River, which is linked with the River Elbe. Details of these earliest arrivals are disclosed in the locally excavated Stone Age remains, including tools and jewels.

Celtic tribesmen settled in the area well over two thousand years ago, followed by a Germanic people. However, of more lasting significance, the first Slavs—ancestors of the Czechs—arrived in the fifth or sixth century A.D., choosing hilltops for safety.

The second half of the ninth century saw the construction of the original fortifications of the castle. It was from here that the Czechs were ruled by the members of the Přemyslid family, a dynasty going back to mythical roots and forward well into the Middle Ages.

A Saintly Pioneer

Methodius, a Greek preacher, has been greatly credited for bringing Christianity to the Slavs during the late ninth century. This erudite itinerant, the "Apostle of the Slavs," set an example for the ordinary citizens when he baptized Prince Borivoj circa 873. Methodius went on to be declared a true saint, as was Borivoj's widow, Ludmilla. This devout Christian woman was assassinated, the victim of a pagan cabal. Many a royal murder was to follow, but the steadfast Ludmilla was assured her place as patron saint of Bohemia.

The grandson of Ludmilla, the first of the rulers named Wenceslas (*Václav* in Czech), held the stage relatively briefly in the tenth century. During his reign a church dedicated to St. Vitus was built at Prague Castle. Wenceslas, who was a fervent believer, became the first of the Czech princes to be murdered in the job—he was ambushed on his way to mass. It was a family affair in the classic mould, a combination of jealousy, religious disagreement, and political greed. The killer was his younger brother, Boleslav, known as the Cruel.

Far from being condemned for eliminating the now sainted Wenceslas, Boleslav assumed power and held it for

The view from Charles Bridge, a survey of architectural style, from Gothic spires to Baroque masterpieces.

nearly half a century. During his long reign a well-travelled Jewish merchant, Ibrahim ibn Jacob, wrote admiringly of Prague as a great and busy trading centre with solid buildings of stone. The town became a bishopric in 973; the monastery of St. George was established on Castle Hill at this time.

Early on in the 11th century Přemyslid rule was extended to neighbouring Moravia by Břetislav I, the great-grandson of Boleslav. He went on to become a vassal of the German emperor, opening the door to centuries of German influence. Břetislav's son, Vratislav II, was the first monarch to bear the title of King of Bohemia.

More Wenceslases

Among kings, namesakes are about as common as jesters, but the Wenceslas saga is more than usually confusing. Prince Wenceslas I, the saint, was not the only Wenceslas I. The second Wenceslas I became King of Bohemia in 1230, and ruled long and well. Encouraging the arts, he presided over a growing prosperity—and population. Since the early 13th century, immigrants from Germany had been moving into Bohemia and some settled in Prague. In 1257, King Otakar II founded the Lesser Quarter as a German enclave, protected by German law.

Wenceslas II, Otakar's son, was notable for his diplomatic skills, but there was nothing very diplomatic about the way he dealt with a threat to his power from his opportunistic stepfather; Wenceslas had the old man executed. Thanks to large finds of silver at this time the economy boomed, and the Prague *groschen* became a stable international currency.

The dynasty's luck eventually ran out with the son of Wenceslas II. In the summer of 1306, early in his reign, the teenaged king was assassinated in Moravia. The killer was never found, and Wenceslas III went down in history as the last of the Přemyslid kings.

The Great Charles

Another Wenceslas grew up to be the king who transformed Prague from a provincial town into an important world capital. As a young man, gaining a good education in Paris, this prince chose to become an ex-Wenceslas, and changed his name to Charles.

He was the son of John (Jan) of Luxembourg, a man of action who ruled Bohemia for 36 years. Wenceslas/Charles gave his name for France, but his francophile father gave his life. King John was killed in 1346, at an early stage in the

---

Czech Republic in Perspective

Geography: Landlocked in Central Europe, the Czech Republic is bordered by Poland, Germany, Austria, and Slovakia. Its area is 78,864 sq km (30,449 sq miles), about one-sixth the size of Spain. Highest point: Snéžka in the Giant Mountains, 1,602 meters (5,255 feet) above sea level.

Population: About 10.3 million.

Government: Parlimentary democracy, replacing more than 40 years of communist rule.

Industry: Formerly geared to Comecon economics, the Czech Republic's industries now include fuel; metallurgy; car, machinery, and equipment manufacture; glass; leather; and armaments. Agriculture produces grains, sugar beets, potatoes.

Religion: Most churches are Roman Catholic.

Language: Czech.

Hundred Years' War, whilst fighting on the losing side at the Battle of Crécy.

Even before his coronation, the future King, Charles IV, was deeply involved in running Prague and Bohemia. His relations with the church were always warm, and in 1344 he convinced the pope to promote Prague to an archbishopric. Under his direction, centuries of work began on the present St. Vitus Cathedral, the resplendent Gothic centrepiece of Hradčany Castle. Early in his reign Charles acted to put Prague firmly on the intellectual map of the world. In 1348 he founded Central Europe's first university. He expanded the city to the New Town, thus providing room for useful immigrants from all over Europe—artists, craftsmen, and merchants. Prague then became the world's fourth-biggest city in area. Not far from town he built Karlštejn Castle, to keep the crown jewels out of harm's way. Finally, he gave Prague its Gothic bridge, the Charles Bridge, which is still a useful and beautiful link between the Old Town and Lesser Quarter after more than 600 years of torrents and flood.

In 1355 Charles added yet another historic title to his regalia when he was crowned Holy Roman Emperor. Back in Prague he ruled nobly over the empire, as well as Bohemia, until his death in 1378.

Religious Strife

The city of Prague should have thrived as the administrative headquarters of the empire that Charlemagne had started, but people and events conspired against it. Charles IV's son and successor, Wenceslas IV, turned out to be the wrong man for the job. He might have proved adequate in quieter times, but his reign was marred by feuds, revolts, and wars. A most irresolute leader, Wenceslas turned his back on distant problems, and even ignored some crises in Prague itself. The Holy

Roman Empire deposed him, and on the home front he was the target of a couple of palace coups.

In the most momentous crisis that Wenceslas failed to address, Prague lived through the first skirmishes of a prelude to the Reformation. At Prague's Bethlehem Chapel a priest, theologian, and professor named Jan Hus challenged the excesses of the Catholic church of the day and demanded it change its ways. Hus's demands for reform became so vigorous that he was excommunicated, then arrested for heresy, and finally burned at the stake in 1415. Czech nationalists and religious reformers far beyond Prague never forgot him. Wenceslas IV, who had started out as a lukewarm supporter of reform, failed to save Hus's life.

Statuary on Charles Bridge testifies to the important role of religion in the city's history.

The movement went marching on with ever wider popular support, much to the dismay of the Papacy. In 1419 a reformist mob invaded Prague's New Town Hall, liberated imprisoned Hussites, and threw several Catholic city councillors from the windows. History calls this event the First Defenestration of Prague. It was to be the start of a long tradition. In Prague, throwing officials out of office could mean quite literally throwing them out of the window.

The harried brother of the unfortunate Wenceslas, King Sigismund, marshalled all the Czech Catholic forces and foreign allies in a crusade against the Hussites. The rebels, however, fought back. Their under-equipped but highly motivated peasant army won some noteworthy victories, defeating Sigismund at the Battle of Vítkov Hill and other foes farther afield. The rebels were commanded by a brilliant one-eyed soldier, Jan Žižka, who invented a new kind of warfare, improvising a mobile artillery force on armoured farm wagons. In spite of the success of his roving cannonry it was another two centuries before conventional armies followed Žižka's lead. Eventually, and inevitably, the rebels were defeated, but their saga is still richly remembered today in the Czech Republic.

The monarchy entered a crisis when Sigismund died without leaving a clear successor. His son-in-law, Albrecht of Austria, was thrust into the gap but soon died. Awkwardly, Albrecht's only son was born after his father's death; he was known by the unfortunate title Ladislas Posthumous. Though his claim to the throne was successful, the boy's career was cut short. Rumours long persisted that Posthumous had been murdered, though a more recent investigation suggested natural causes. The alleged poisoner was a dynamic politician by the name of George of Poděbrady, who, in spite of all the bad publicity, was elected to succeed him.

George aligned himself with the Hussites, to the great displeasure of the neighbour-

Flanked by figures representing Vanity and Death, Prague's Astronomical Clock has been telling time since the 15th century.

ing Catholic kings and the papacy. He was eventually excommunicated and boycotted, which wasn't good for Prague's business. Even though a rival king disputed his throne, George refused to quit. He died, peacefully, while still in office.

Four Habsburg Centuries

Absentee kings had absent-mindedly ruled Bohemia from George's death until 1526, when the Habsburgs claimed the throne. But even these serious monarchs were too busy with their responsibilities elsewhere in the Holy Roman Empire —for instance, fighting off the galloping advance of the Turkish army—to accomplish much in Prague. Mostly they tried to cope with Bohemia's grave religious divisions. By now the Protestant faith had become a powerful influence; but the Habsburgs remained zealous Catholics.

The nicest thing the eccentric Emperor Rudolph II did for Bohemia was to move his capital from Vienna to Prague. Under this imperial impulse the arts and sciences reached newer heights, and splendid Renaissance buildings further beautified the city. The emperor, though centuries ahead of his time, was also psychologically disturbed. This encouraged his political opponents to slowly whittle away at his authority. The principal accomplishment of his reign (1576–1611) was a decree which granted freedom of religion to all Catholics and Protestants alike. However, the Catholic king, Ferdinand II, did not honour it. This served to exacerbate the inherent religious conflict which soon escalated into the suffering of the Thirty Years' War.

One of the first incidents in the violent struggle was another of those Prague defenestrations. This time the window was in the Bohemian Chancellery of Prague Castle, and the victims were a couple of governors and their secretary, all accused of anti-Protestant actions. Remarkably, though, they recovered from this incident.

In the rebellion that ensued, Ferdinand was deposed, but his supporters rallied and, with a lot of help from elsewhere in the empire, triumphed in the Battle of the White Mountain, fought on Prague's doorstep.

Restored to power, Ferdinand sent persuasive messages about loyalty to the populace: he had a couple of dozen rebel leaders executed in the Old Town Square. Roman Catholicism was proclaimed the only legal religion, eliminating any theological subtleties.

Ferdinand's decisive victory radically changed the face of Prague, haggard as it was after the fighting, and stripped of its role as the imperial capital. A large majority of Protestant landowners emigrated to more welcoming climes, and their property went to Ferdinand's Catholic supporters. Those remaining were forced to convert to Catholicism. Baroque architecture, typical of the sort favoured in Catholic Italy, became the fashion, and the medieval atmosphere of Prague gave way to grand, extravagant 17th-century palaces and a parade of Baroque churches signalling the great triumph of the Counter-Reformation.

Looking out over Prague's ancient roofscape from Charles Bridge—the view hasn't altered much over the centuries.

Henceforward, German, not Czech, was spoken in palace and courthouse. The tensions that grew up between Prague's German and Czech-speaking citizens would persist well into the 20th century.

Maria Theresa and Son

Maria Theresa, the daughter, wife, and mother of Holy Roman emperors, was the only queen to have reigned over Prague. In between diplomatic engagements she produced 16 children, including Marie Antoinette, the future Queen of France. Prague's citizens were fertile as well; during her long rule the population grew to more than 80,000.

Under her son and heir, Joseph II, religious toleration was restored. Joseph also abolished serfdom and relaxed censorship. On the municipal level, he consolidated the city of Prague from its previous four components—Hradčany, Lesser Quarter, Old Town, and New Town. Music provides a gauge of the cultural development of Joseph's Prague: in 1787 Mozart was invited to conduct the world premiere of *Don Giovanni* in the Estates Theatre. It was a hit, though critics in Vienna later panned the opera. Mozart always appreciated Prague's good taste.

Industrial Prague

By the middle of the 19th century, Prague's population had exceeded 100,000. Factories were built and a railway line opened between Vienna and Prague, signalling the start of the Industrial Revolution. Bohemia went on to become the most advanced manufacturing centre of the Austrian Empire.

Another kind of revolution started in 1848, uniting Czech nationalists and the new working class of Prague against the overlords in Vienna; Marxist historians called it the "bourgeois revolution." The remote, rigid Austrian authorities soon extinguished the uprising, but not the smouldering nationalist feelings of the Czechs. When Prague's monumental National Theatre opened in 1881, the first work ever performed was a new opera by Smetana, a proud and patriotic saga called *Libuše*. Dvořák, too, took his inspiration from Czech folk songs. Nationalist Prague was conspicuously out of step with the rhythm of the capital, Vienna, the home of the waltz.

The 20th Century

When the heir to the Habsburg throne, Archduke Franz Ferdinand, was assassinated in June 1914, the Austro-Hungarian Empire was plunged into the tragic carnage of World War I. Prague was put under a state of emergency and its young men were shipped off to fight for the Kaiser in Czech-speaking units. In the meantime, the Bolshevik Revolution in Russia sent ripples to Prague and beyond, though the Communist Party of Czechoslovakia wasn't founded until 1921.

From the dusty ashes of the defeated Austria-Hungary, an independent Czechoslovakian republic was proclaimed in October 1918. Prague was the capital of the First Republic, comprising Bohemia, Moravia, and Slovakia. The first president was Tomáš G. Masaryk, a widely travelled and admired philosophy professor, who was re-elected three times. He died in 1937, before the agony of yet another European war.

Czechoslovakia was at the centre of the storm that blew up into World War II. In September 1938, six months after the annexation of Austria, Hitler demanded self-determination for Czechoslovakia's German-speaking citizens. To try to appease him, Britain and France handed over the country's western provinces to the Third Reich at a great-powers conference held in Munich. Czechoslovakia was further diminished when Poland and Hungary rushed in with territorial claims of their own. Then Hitler threatened to rain bombs on Prague unless the remains of the country were made a German protectorate. The government of what remained of Czechoslovakia's Second Republic capitulated. Six long years of occupation were to follow.

In May 1945, the resistance forces in Prague led an insurrection against the Germans. The rebels held out for four days until Soviet troops liberated the capital, opening a new era. When parliamentary elections were held a year later, the communists won nearly 40 percent of the votes. The non-communist pre-war president Edvard Beneš, elected again, invited the veteran communist leader Klement Gottwald to form a coalition cabinet.

Gottwald, who had spent the war years in the Soviet Union, seized his big chance in 1948. When several non-communist ministers resigned in protest against his one-sided policies, Gottwald packed the government with supporters. Beneš bowed to the power play, but he refused to sign a new constitution that the communists steamrollered through parliament, and consequently resigned. Beneš, who had suffered two strokes, soon died of natural causes, a few months after his defenestrated foreign minister, Jan Masaryk.

Gottwald, as the new president, framed a five-year economic plan, cracked down on the churches, and purged his opponents outside and inside the party. Scores of political figures were executed, and thousands arrested. Gottwald died suddenly in 1953, a few days after attending the funeral of his old mentor, Stalin. The show trials went on under Antonín Novotný, while farmers were forced into collectives and the arts were smothered under harsh Socialist Realism.

A reform movement in the late 1960s culminated in the "Prague Spring" under Alexander Dubček, the head of the Slovak communist party. Unshackling the press and the arts, Dubček promised "socialism with a human face." But this was 20 years too early. On 21 August 1968, reform was crushed by the armed forces of the Soviet Union, ostensibly there by invitation, and assisted by Poland, Bulgaria, East Germany, and Hungary. As the rest of the world watched Soviet tanks rumbling through Wenceslas Square, Prague wept.

New Challenges

The new party chiefs turned, with limited success, to economic development, maintaining hardline traditions even when the winds of change finally blew in from Moscow.

In 1989, Wenceslas Square was again the scene of repression: television showed the police clubbing peaceful students who demonstrated for an end to one-party rule. This time the long-suffering citizens had had enough. Now Prague's seemingly invincible communist regime cringed before the loud voice of the people. The playwright, Václav Havel, called it the "velvet revolution."

Dubček, rehabilitated, was elected chairman of a rejuvenated parliament. Meanwhile, Havel, an ex-dissident freshly out of jail, was sentenced to a term in the castle, as the nation's president by acclamation.

In June 1992, parliamentary elections were won by the Civil Democratic Party and Václav Klaus became Prime Minister of the Czech cabinet. In the meantime, Václav Havel renounced his position as federal president. Near the end of the year, tensions between Czechs (including Moravians and Silesians) and Slovaks, which had been threatening to split the country in two, finally resulted in that division.

On 1 January 1993, Czechoslovakia was peaceably divided into the Czech and Slovak Republics, and in February of that same year Václav Havel was returned to power as the President of the new Czech Republic.

WHERE TO GO

Since the days of Charles IV Prague has consisted of four main areas, each with its own distinctive character. Two elements of the equation can be found on each side of the ever-present Vltava River. The most monumental portion, on the heights overlooking the rest of the city, is Hradčany, the ancient district featuring Prague Castle. Beneath it, the charming Lesser Quarter (*Malá Strana* in Czech, which literally means Small Side) was established in the 13th century. Across the river, the Old Town (*Staré Město*) is one of Europe's best-preserved medieval capitals, including remarkable vestiges of the Jewish ghetto. Next to the Old Town, the (relatively) New Town (*Nové Město*) is rich in parks, gardens, and Gothic and Baroque architecture (Prague's Baroque buildings have enough caryatids to hold up a medium-sized town all by themselves).

You can get a good idea of the city's geography and character on a guided coach tour, but then you should switch to the most gratifying sightseeing plan: exploring the city, neighourhood by neighourhood, on foot. Once you have tackled the highlights, try to squeeze in an excursion or two to the Bohemian countryside and its grand castles.

CASTLE DISTRICT

From across the river, Prague's "Enchanted Castle" looks like a sweeping cliff crowned with palaces, topped in unequivocal glory by the spires of a great cathedral. A thousand years ago, the bulwarks were of mud, and the church was a primitive round chapel. However, one thing about the fortress hasn't changed. As it was in the age of Prague's first prince, the castle remains the home of the country's political chieftain, now titled the President of the Czech Republic.

The castle has become the scene of increasing commercial activity due to continuous efforts to open up more of its treasures to the public and to begin to reverse the many years of neglect. Much, of course, depends on funding, and it will probably be quite some time before visitors can experience all the benefits.

You can enter the castle compound from three different directions—the north, east, or west. Excursion parties generally approach from the west, then proceed on foot through the enclave and depart, an hour or two later, through the eastern ramparts. In the following pages, we will follow the same general itinerary. There is one advantage when walking from west to east: it's all downhill.

A soaring clock tower—its carillon of 27 bells plays an hourly hymn—introduces one the most impressive Baroque structures in Prague, a great shrine called simply **Loreta** (Our Lady of Loreto). Situated on the edge of Prague Castle, this elaborate set of cloisters is fronted by a stately and handsome 18th-century façade.

At the centre of a grassy courtyard rather cluttered with statuary is the "casa santa" (1626), a representation of the house in Nazareth where, according to tradition, the Virgin Mary was born. Angels were said to have carried it to the Italian town of Loreto, now a major shrine. This is one of dozens of copies of the house that were built in Bohemia to rally the country's peasants to the Counter-Reformation. Another attraction inside Loreta is the Church of the Nativity (*kostel Narození Páně*), a small, lavishly decorated 18th-century church with over 120 exquisitely sculpted angels in its interior.

The **treasury,** upstairs in the cloister, glitters with precious reliquaries, monstrances, and mitres, all very clearly displayed with captions in English, French, and German as well as Czech. Pride of place goes to a monstrance from Vienna, dated 1699, encrusted with thousands of diamonds.

Černin Palace (*Černínský palác*), across the wide square from the Loreta, has a monumental Baroque façade extending for 150 meters (492 feet). Built by a noble diplomat in the 17th century, the palace was recruited as a barracks in the middle of the 19th century. The palace has now been restored to its former elegance, and serves modern diplomacy as the Czech Republic's Ministry of Foreign Affairs.

Hračany Square

Hradčany Square (*Hradčanské náměstí*), an irregular-looking medieval town square, leads to the entrance of Prague Castle. Although the centuries have changed its face, it is still full of historical flourishes.

Notice the Baroque **plague column,** erected by the grateful survivors of an epidemic in the early 18th century. Earlier, the less lucky leaders of the 1547 uprising were executed here for failing to overthrow King Ferdinand I.

On the west side of the square, the **Tuscan Palace** (*Toskánský palác*) is typical of the splendour of late-17th-century Baroque. The coats of arms of the Dukes of Tuscany, who used to own the building, can still be seen on the façade.

To its right, the former **Martinic Palace** (*Martinický palác*) was built around 1570 in the Renaissance style. The exterior decorations still feature coloured *sgraffito* ("scratched" plaster) illustrations of mythological and biblical stories. In the interior, which is now used for concerts and exhibitions, there is a main hall with a painted-wood ceiling, a courtyard with more *sgraffitia,* and a chapel displaying paintings.

The **Archepiscopal Palace** (*Arcibiskupský palác*) has developed through several different stages, most significantly the late-17th-century Baroque, to which Rococo details were later added. The public has one chance each year to view its exuberant interior, on the Thursday before Easter. Behind the archbishop's palace, the former **Sternberg Palace** (*Šternberský palác*) houses the European art collection of the **National Gallery.** (A full description of Prague's museums starts on page 66.)

Finally, take a close look at the former **Schwarzenberg Palace** (*Schwarzenberský palác*), a Renaissance triumph from the middle of the 16th century. The windows on each floor are a different shape, and the façade is decorated with striking *sgraffito* effects simulating rows of facets spiking from the walls. Restored soon after World War II, the palace now houses Prague's **Military History Museum,** which covers around five thousand years.

☞ Prague Castle

In the Czech Republic, a castle may mean a fortress, or a Disneyesque turreted building, or a walled complex of contiguous, often fanciful structures. Prague Castle (*Pražský hrad*) is a city in itself, in the manner of Granada's Alhambra or Moscow's Kremlin, though it is centuries older than either of them. However you go about it, a tour of Prague Castle, with its array of churches, palaces, towers, museums, and gardens, involves a great deal of walking.

Facing Hradčany Square, the ceremonial entrance to this encyclopaedia of history and architecture is guarded by a couple of white-gloved army sentries standing to attention on either side of the main gate. Above them, outsized statues of mythological giants using both dagger and bludgeon to despatch their foes are modern copies of Ignaz Platzer's 18th-century originals. Don't let them put you off.

Once through the gate you are in the First Courtyard (*první nádvoří*) of the castle, an 18th-century afterthought. As you walk on through the **Matthias Gate** (*Matyášova brána*), a Baroque triumphal arch, you will see glass doors which lead to the headquarters of the Czech president.

Built over an ancient moat, the Second Courtyard (*druhé nádvoří*) is much larger and older than the first. In the northwest corner, there is a modern museum, the **Prague Castle Picture Gallery,** with a fine selection of Old Masters. Before it went highbrow, this part of the castle was a stable. To the south, the **Holy Cross chapel** (*kaple svatého Kříže*) now contains objects from the treasury of St. Vitus Cathedral, including a coat of mail said to have belonged to Good King Wenceslas.

In the biggest enclave of all, the **Third Courtyard** (*třetí nádvoří*), stands the grandest sight of all: **St. Vitus Cathedral**

The St. Vitus Cathedral is just one section of the Prague Castle complex.

(*katedrála svatého Víta*). Its majestic western façade calls to mind Nôtre-Dame in Paris, but the truth is that this part is 19th-century neo-Gothic. In fact, Prague's biggest church was one thousand years in the making.

The original church on this site was first ordered by Prince Wenceslas in the early tenth century, well before he was promoted to saint. The present building began in the reign of the enterprising Emperor Charles IV. The first of several generations of architects to be involved was a 14th-century Frenchman, Matthias of Arras, who was succeeded by Peter Parler, a prolific German architect and sculptor, and his two sons. The whole project was finally completed in 1929.

The **south façade** of the cathedral is decorated with hundreds of years of inspiring art. Over the porch is a much-restored 14th-century mosaic of the *Last Judgement*, including contemporary portraits of Charles IV and one of his queens, Elizabeth of Pomerania. Look up to your left at the superb gold-filigreed Renaissance grillework in the great Gothic window. Above is a pair of single-handed clocks, the one above indicating the hour and the one beneath, the quarter-hour. Complementing all these features is the delicate tracery, as intricate as the leaves on a tree.

Inside the cathedral the most beautiful of the many chapels is dedicated to the Saint Wenceslas. Peter Parler designed and adorned it during the middle of the 14th century, some 400 years after the murder of the young prince. Nearer to the high altar, there is a stairway from the Holy Cross Chapel to the burial vault, where you can see the tombs of some of the most distinguished royal personages, as well as portions of the original Romanesque church dating from the tenth century. Otherwise, there is much to admire as you explore this cathedral, from its Gothic oratory to the Renaissance pulpit to the 20th-century stained-glass windows.

Just north of the cathedral, the **Powder Tower** (*Mihulka*) was part of the castle's 15th-century defences. Restored in more modern times, the circular tower has become a small museum. The ground floor covers all the military aspects of the tower, and upstairs there is an exhibition of Renaissance science and technology. In the basement, an exposition of metal casting recalls the 16th century, when this tower was used as a foundry.

The **Old Royal Palace** (*Starý Královský palác*) is the secular equivalent of the huge cathedral—a medieval striving for grandeur in stone. It was home to the kings of Bohemia until the 16th century, when the Habsburgs turned it into offices and warehouses.

The palace's Vladislav Hall (*Vladislavský sǎl*), regal in its design and dimensions, was begun in 1493. The architect, Benedikt Ried, was knighted for his great achievement. It is known as the largest secular hall built without the support of either dome or pillars during the Middle Ages. Tournaments were held here, with up to one hundred horsemen taking part; today's tourists depart down the staircase designed for the horses. The hall's intertwining ribbon vaults, 13 meters (43 feet) high, add grace to the pompous setting. Imagine a throng of subjects all gath-

Light through lofty stained-glass windows illuminates the interior of St. Vitus Cathedral.

ered here to pay homage to their king, or for a plenary meeting of the lords.

For a couple of hundred years the province of Bohemia was governed from the **Bohemian Chancellery** (*Česká kancelář*), just off Vladislav Hall. In the second, smaller room, the citizens refined the concept of the window of opportunity. History was made here with a splash in 1618 when two governors and their clerk were defenestrated (see page 17). It's a long way down, but they survived.

Diagonally across the vast Vladislav Hall, the **Hall of the Diet** (*Stará sněmovna*) exudes medieval dignity. The supreme court used to sit here—note the paintings of Habsburg kings.

Founded in the early tenth century, **St. George's basilica** (*bazilika svatého Jiří*) is considered to be Prague's oldest surviving church. Sighting its ochre Baroque façade, facing St. George's Square, you would never guess there's an attractively restored Romanesque church inside. Here you'll see the tombs of Prince Vratislav,

Stepping into the castle courtyards is like taking a journey into the past.

the founder of the church, and of Boleslav II (known as the Pious). The 13th-century wall paintings are some of Prague's oldest. Next door, the former tenth-century **Convent of St. George** (*Jiřský klášter*) was the Czech Republic's first convent, dissolved in 1782 by Emperor Joseph II. Now belonging to the National Gallery, it contains the peerless **Collection of Old Bohemian Art** (see page 66).

A final major attraction in the castle is the **Golden Lane** (*Zlatá ulička*), a narrow cul-de-sac (dead-end street) with irresistible pastel houses. During the 16th century these tiny houses, built into the ramparts, were occupied by archers defending the castle. Later on, a number of artisans both lived and worked here, among them goldsmiths (hence the name of the street). Now most of the houses are **souvenir shops.**

Strahov Monastery

Amidst tall trees on the hill southwest of the Castle district is the architectural complex of the Strahov Monastery (*Strahovský klášter*), founded in 1140. The original wooden building, put up for the just-organized Premonstratensian order, was soon replaced by a more substantial Romanesque

Prague Castle, which can be seen from many points throughout the city, is practically a city in itself.

structure. It was much more elaborate than the castle itself, but, sadly, it burned down. The monastery's Gothic and Renaissance successors gave way to a Baroque facelift. However, some precious early aspects have been preserved.

Apart from the two Baroque churches (one has been converted to an exhibition hall), the monastery is remarkable for its lavish **library;** its vaulted ceilings and stucco ornaments are overwhelming. There are, in fact, two collections of books, one devoted to philosophy and the other to theology. Now both form part of the **National Literature Memorial.** The ceiling frescoes are well worth admiring.

LESSER QUARTER

For Baroque charm, no area of Prague is such an unalloyed delight as the Lesser Quarter (*Malá Strana*). Rising, imperceptibly at first, from the riverside to Hradčany, this is the second-oldest part of the city. The street plan dates from the middle of the 13th century and the reign of Otakar II, who encouraged German immigrants to settle here. But Malá Strana rarely looks its age, as almost every monument of the early days was wiped out by a series of fires in the Middle Ages. The district was subsequently rebuilt during the Renaissance and then Baroque periods, with a stately but intimate appeal.

In this section, we begin to explore Malá Strana from the riverside, a most attractive approach, especially as it means crossing Prague's Vltava River via its most splendid bridge.

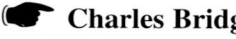

Charles Bridge

For the Holy Roman Emperor, Charles IV, the bridge that now bears his name was a utilitarian project. In the 14th century the townsfolk simply needed a solid stone link above flood level. In 1870, what had previously been called the

Prague Bridge or the Stone Bridge was renamed, in his honour, the Charles Bridge (*Karlův most*). By that time, the trusty Gothic structure had acquired more intricate Baroque adornments, to make it a most exhilarating work of art.

Due to some complications during construction and reconstruction, the bridge is not the shortest distance between two points; here and there its path veers slightly, as if the blueprints had become wrinkled. Although still wide enough to carry motor traffic, it's been reserved for pedestrians only since 1950. Stroll across at a leisurely pace, and stop now and again to admire the view from, and of, the bridge.

Starting from the east (Old Town) side of the river: the bridge is buttressed by a great Gothic **tower** massive enough to daunt almost any prospective invader. Both architect and sculptor, Peter Parler was responsible for this innovation, as well as the interesting statues thereon of his sponsors, Charles IV and Wenceslas IV (seated), and the patron of the bridge, St. Vitus.

Charles Bridge is quietest at dawn, when crowds have dispersed and early-birds can contemplate the architectural detail at their leisure.

There are 30 **statues** or sculptural groups that line Charles Bridge, with 15 on each side. Dating primarily from the 18th and 19th centuries, each one has a history behind it. On the right, the Crucifixion scene (1667) is in fact the oldest statue on the bridge. It includes a large 17th-century Hebrew inscription, paid for by a rich Jew accused of blasphemy. Midway across the bridge, the statue cast in bronze honours a local martyr, St. John of Nepomuk, tossed into the Vltava in 1393.

Beyond it, on the opposite side, an 18th-century statue movingly portrays St. Luitgard kissing the wounds of Christ. The next-to-last sculptural ensemble on the left offers a most horrific view of captive Christians, guarded by a bored Turkish jailer armed with a scimitar and barbed whip.

In some of the niches beneath the sculptures, artists sell their paintings and drawings of the bridge and the city—or propose an instant portrait of any passing tourist or patron of the arts.

Finding your way around the Lesser Quarter is easy, and Charles Bridge is an excellent place to stop and study the view—or the map.

The Left Bank

Guarding the western end of the bridge are two Gothic towers connected by an arch, the **Malá Strana Gate.** The ensemble was begun late in the 12th century. It is here that **Mostecká Street** begins—a narrow shopping street lined with fine Baroque houses. It was part of the King's Road, the route of coronation processions. For a brief diversion, turn left into Lázeňská Street, which leads to a distinguished neighbourhood. Both Peter the Great and Chateaubriand used to stay in the former hotel at number 6.

A Maltese cross marks the **church of the Virgin Below the Chain** (*kostel Panny Marie pod řetězem*), originally a 12th-century basilica which once belonged to the Knights of Malta. The Baroque palaces which face **Knights of Malta Square** (*Maltézské náměstí*) house a library, the Japanese embassy, and a cabaret show.

You'd hardly know the low-lying district of **Kampa** was an island, but it is separated from the "mainland" of Malá Strana by a narrow arm of the Vltava that was once used to power watermills. Although no single building stands out, most of the Baroque houses here contribute to an all-round air of dignity and good taste.

The bustling atmosphere today in busy Karmelitská Street is a far, noisy cry from the contemplative scene chosen by the Carmelites for their convent. The **church of Our Lady of Victory** (*kostel Panny Marie Vítězné*) was the city's first Baroque building. Construction began in 1611; it served as a Protestant church until the barefoot Carmelites took it over several years later. The main attraction of this church is a Renaissance **statuette** of the "Holy Infant of Prague." It was brought to Prague from Spain in the mid-17th century.

Up the Hill

From many parts of Prague you can see an unlikely silhouette on the horizon—a copy of the Eiffel Tower. The local version is less than one-fifth the size of the original, but its site on Petřín Hill adds to its stature. The **Petřín Lookout** (*Petřínská rozhledna*) was built for the Prague Industrial Exhibition of 1891, only two years after Gustav Eiffel's engineering exploit had amazed Paris. Inevitably, in recent times it was commandeered as a television transmitting tower. In the same area of parkland you'll find an astronomical observatory, a panoramic restaurant, three venerable churches, and a relic of the 1891 fair—a maze built of mirrors.

A favourite way to reach Petřín Hill is still by funicular (*lanová dráha*). To locate the cable-propelled train's Malá Strana terminal, follow the red signs along Újezd Street.

A view of the Lesser Quarter, with its age-old architecture, located on the Vltava River.

Lesser Quarter Square

Strolling through the pedestrian zone of Prague Castle may have spoiled you for the main square of the Lesser Quarter, **Malostranské náměstí.** The pressure of traffic now detracts from the flavour of its fine old arcaded buildings.

Looming over it all is the massive dome and bell tower of Prague's greatest Baroque church, **St. Nicholas** (*kostel svatého Mikuláše*). The architect was the prolific Bavarian Christoph Dientzenhofer; after his death his very talented son, Kilian Ignaz, continued the project and added the dome. This was originally a Jesuit church, designed to display the order's power after the success of the Counter-Reformation. However, soon after it was finished the Jesuits were dissolved by Pope Clement XIV, and St. Nicholas was confiscated for use as a parish church.

The church's interior is a sumptuous anthology of religious art, topped by one of the biggest ceiling **frescoes** in Europe. The artist, Jan Lukáš Kracker, covered 1,500 square metres (1,794 square yards) with scenes from the life of St. Nicholas. Beneath the dome, surrounded by giant statues of saints, the crucifix on the main altar is scarcely bigger than you'd find on the wall of a monk's cell.

Behind St. Nicholas Church, the other, much busier, part of the square is lined with substantial buildings linked by an arcade. Notable is the former **Lesser**

Cultural attractions can be in the unlikeliest of places.

Keeping time, Prague style. An old timepiece in the tower of Old Town Square.

Quarter Town Hall (*Malostranská radnice*), now functioning as a nightclub.

St. Thomas Church (*kostel svatého Tomáše*) is just around the corner. It was later given a Baroque facelift in the early part of the 18th century by the younger Dientzenhofer.

Letenská Street leads to the rear of Prague's most luxurious palace, and the way in to the Wallenstein Garden (*Valdštejnská zahrada*), open daily to the public from May to September. These formal gardens, as big as a city park, were laid out in the early 17th century, an Italian Baroque whim designed to impress the neighbours. The main avenue of the park is lined with statues which are, in fact, copies of the 17th-century originals by the expatriate Dutch sculptor

Number, Please

Don't let the street numbers of Prague drive you up the wall.

Most buildings have two kinds of numbers prominently affixed. The blue plaque announces the normal street number; if you're looking for 24 Somewhere Street, you'll find it (in blue) next to number 22. But house 22 may also have a big red plaque reading "19," while house 24, next door, bears the red number "162." The red numbers, non-geographical, indicate the order in which the buildings entered the municipal register; the lower the number in red, the older the house.

Adriaen de Vries. The garden makes a truly delightful setting for summer plays and music concerts. The main part of the palace is currently closed to the public while restoration work is in progress.

The man who built the palace, known as Generalissimo Albrecht Wenzel Eusebius von Wallenstein, also known here as von Waldstein, came to an unhappy end. When the rich and politically potent Wallenstein decided to try for the throne of Bohemia, the incumbent emperor, Ferdinand II, frowned on his conspiracy and ordered his assassination. The German poet Schiller, some 166 years later, chose the Wallenstein saga as the subject of his most powerful play.

OLD TOWN

From Prague's earliest days, its strategic importance in the centre of Europe has been evident to friend and foe. While power was barricaded in the castle on the hill, rough-and-ready commerce animated the oppo-site bank of the Vltava, at the junction of the traditional trading routes link-ing Europe's east, west, north, and south. It was only a few centuries be-fore the teeming market place evolved

> Black market money changers are common, but unofficial money changing is illegal.

into a distinguished main square from which a jumble of historic streets radiate. Prague's Old Town (*Staré Město*) has more medieval delights and Baroque surprises than you can take in at a single survey. Start your journey at the ancient crossroads.

Hub of Old Town

In an irregular open space as vast as Red Square in Moscow, **Old Town Square** (*Staroměstské náměstí*) provides a daz-zling panorama. Stand in the middle and turn a slow circle:

it's as if all the most charming city streets of Europe were stretched around you. Vying for the most beautiful superlatives, every building is different in every detail—roofs, windows, doors, and colours from the most unconventional, yet pleasing palette: tangerine and pistachio, apple red and lime green. In central Prague, you can get your bearings from two sets of towers overlooking this low-rise scene. The multi-turreted twin towers to the east belong to the Týn church, while the Gothic clock tower of the medieval town hall is at the southwest corner.

The urban panorama is interrupted to the north by a mighty **monument** to Jan Hus, teacher, preacher, and martyr. It was officially dedicated in 1915 on the 500th anniversary of the reformer's execution by fire for heresy. Sculpted by Ladislav Šaroun, the inscription reads, "Truth will prevail."

The **Old Town Hall** (*Staroměstská radnice*), begun in the 14th century, has developed in slow stages to match the municipality's growth in size and importance. Neighbouring houses were incorporated, while additions and modifications continued to be made until the 19th century, as if generations of "do-it-yourself" enthusiasts had started a tradition of expanding and improving the old family house. However, the structure suffered quite badly during World War II, and restoration on the east wing has only recently been completed.

The most obvious highlight of the Old Town Hall is its **astronomical clock** (circa 1480). Every hour on the hour, as the crowds in the square look on, intricate clockwork figures on the tower's façade enact a timely story: Death consults his hourglass and yanks a bell cord; Christ and the Apostles appear, while other characters swing into action. Finally, a loud cock crows. Below, an immensely complicated clock tells the time, tracks the movements of the sun and moon (assuming that the earth is the centre of the universe), and displays the 12 signs of the zodiac. The bottom dial indicates the months in pictures. After you have witnessed this spectacle, you can then enter the building for a guided tour. Highlights are the sumptuous **halls** with their 15th-century atmosphere, intricate ceilings, murals and tapestries, and the old **Council Chamber.** Separate entrance fees are charged for the art gallery, the chapel, and the **tower,** from where there is a marvellous view.

Abutting the town hall, on the left side, **Dům U Minuty** is one of Prague's most memorable Renaissance buildings, emblazoned with *sgraffito* decorations on familiar pagan and biblical themes.

On the northeast edge of the square, the former **Goltz-Kinský Palace** dates from the middle of the 18th century. From the statues on the roof to the Rococo embellishments around the windows, it is an outstanding architectural achievement. Like many of the buildings around the square, the palace's basement contains Romanesque remains. The palace now houses the National Gallery's Collection of Graphic Art.

The vibrant pink façade of the Old Town Hall blends in perfectly with its colourful surroundings.

The **Church of Our Lady of Týn** (*kostel Panny Marie před Týnem*) has visibly stood the test of centuries. Notice how some of the exterior walls are faced with stones of many shapes and sizes. The present Gothic church was built in the middle of the 14th century on the old site of a Romanesque structure. This was a church of the reformers even before Jan Hus shook up the religious establishment, but since the Counter-Reformation it has remained a Catholic bastion.

The Týn's twin towers, abristle with turrets, are 80 meters (more than 260 feet) tall. They were built in the 15th and 16th centuries. An even older distinguishing characteristic is the northern portal with a tympanum created at the end of the 14th century by the prolific sculptural workshop of Peter Parler. Inside, the church is filled with Baroque works of art. Facing the main altar, note an interesting **relief** of Tycho Brahe (1546–1601), the talented Danish astronomer and his tomb. As the court astronomer of Rudolph II, Brahe was a leading figure in medieval science. However, he rejected the revolutionary theory of Copernicus, insisting instead that the sun circled the earth.

This monumental memorial to Jan Hus dominates Old Town Square, surrounded by distinctive architectural styles.

Another Old Town church of artistic interest, **St. James's** (*kostel svatého Jakuba*) was founded in 1232, but its ornate appearance dates from the end of the 17th century. St. James's fronts a narrow street northeast of the Týn church, so it's hard to get far away enough from the façade to take in the stucco fantasies of the Italian artist Ottavio Mosto. Fraught with Baroque extravagance, the interior is impressive for its sheer size. St. James's Church is also a treat for the ear, with acclaimed acoustics. On Sundays one of the masses features an orchestra and choir.

An historic street, now reserved for pedestrians, runs to Republic Square from the Old Town Square. **Celetná Street** was part of the long route that was followed by coronation processions from the Powder Tower via the Old Town and Charles Bridge to the castle. The street is lined with grandiose old mansions, mostly Baroque, each worth a close look for the kind of detail that delights the observant eye: the curve of a gable, an unusually shaped window, a wall painting, a statue, or an emblem.

An early-20th-century landmark, a six-storey building in Cubist style, blends in with the rest of Celetná Street, as if taking its cue from the best of Baroque. The **Black Madonna House** (*dům U černé Matky boží*), a Cubist art museum named after the religious statue in a corner niche, can hold its own with any contemporary architecture. Note the big bay windows and the appealing mansard roof.

The Late Gothic **Powder Tower** (*Prašná brána*) takes its name from the gunpowder that was once stored in it. But gunpowder had scarcely been heard of in Europe when the first tower on this site, originally part of the Old Town's defences, was built towards the end of the 13th century. Those were the days of hand-to-hand combats; longer-range service was rendered by spear-throwers and archers. The present tower, surmounting a great ceremonial gateway, was begun in 1475.

The **Municipal House** (*Obecní dům*), alongside, is totally different. Built in the first decade of this century, it is a monument to Art Nouveau style. With recent renovations completed in 1998, the period atmosphere of the bars and restaurants here is attracting visitors again. On this site stood the royal court of Prague, the residence of several Czech rulers.

Just behind this building and the Powder Tower is one of the biggest department stores in Prague, Kotva (The Anchor). It's worth wandering through this 1970s building to size up the capital's standard of living; Kotva sells everything from food to furniture, from toothpaste to souvenirs.

Two buildings now cherished as national cultural monuments are situated in the street known as **Železná** (the name means "iron"), yet another of the interesting historic thoroughfares radiating from the Old Town Square. The home of Charles University, the **Carolinum** (*Karolinum*) was named after Charles IV, who founded it in 1348. Jan Hus served as rector, and after his martyrdom in 1415 the university became a hotbed of the Hussite struggle against the Catholic church.

After the Counter-Reformation triumphed the Carolinum was handed over to the Jesuits. The most pleasing element of the original building still visible is the elegant Gothic **oriel window,** which typically overhangs the street. Also imposing is the huge, high-ceilinged Assembly Hall, built in the 17th century. Most of the remaining complex dates from the 18th century.

With its Neo-Classical façade, the **Estates Theatre** (*Stavovské divadlo*) provides a richly historic setting for great occasions. Since its construction in the 1780s, the theatre has had several names. First it was the Nostič Theatre, and then after World War II it was renamed the Tyl Theatre after a Czech dramatist. The first name of Estates Theatre was restored in 1991. In 1787 the Mozart opera *Don Giovanni* received its world premiere here—Mozart himself conducted the house orchestra. More recently, the theatre's glittering interior was featured in Miloš Forman's film *Amadeus*.

A one-time Carmelite convent in Rytířská Street, a sizeable Baroque presence, used to be the location of the **House of Russian Science and Culture** (*Dům ruské vědy a kultury*). Tourists may well be attracted to the souvenir shop here, selling Russian dolls and records. Just across the street, a late-19th-century palace built in neo-Renaissance style is now the headquarters of the Prague City Savings Bank.

Josefov

Late in the 19th century the city's ancient Jewish ghetto, which was renamed Josefov (Joseph's Town) after Emperor

---

Cubist Architecture

Czech Cubist architecture flourished in multi-faceted originality at the very beginning of the 20th century, but only briefly.

The Black Madonna House (see page 45) is the best-known example. Another first-rate Cubist building is a villa (now an apartment block) facing the river at Rašínovo nábřeží 26. The three-dimensional sculptural effect of the façade carries over into details inside the house.

The same architect, Josef Chochol, created the sizeable Cubist apartment block which occupies a difficult corner site in the Vyšehrad district.

Very few Cubist projects ever got off the drawing board, for tastes soon changed and Prague turned to Modernism.

Joseph II, was bulldozed in the path of a bold urban renewal plan. But stately vestiges of centuries of achievement and turmoil remain, making this an essential part of any tour of the city. Synagogues and an amazing cemetery still survive, surrounded by a neighbourhood of fine Art Nouveau apartment blocks erected on the ruins of the medieval warren. The **Museum of Decorative Arts** backs on to the old ghetto.

Prague's Jewish community can be traced back to the middle of the tenth century. The city's first known synagogue was built in the 12th century but soon burned down. This fate was typical of the ups and violent downs to follow — fires, restrictive laws, and pogroms alternating with periods of relative freedom and creativity. In the 20th century, the vast majority of Prague's Jews were annihilated during World War II according to the Nazi master plan. Ironically, priceless monuments were preserved because Hitler wanted the relics of his victims catalogued. These were meant to have been studied as historical curiosities after the proposed extermination of all Jews.

The fashionable main avenue cutting through the former ghetto is **Pařížská ulice** (Paris Street), where international airlines and tourist agencies have their offices, and boutiques with a foreign flair seem to congregate. The avenue runs from the Old Town Square to the river; directly opposite, high above the river, a lookout platform on top of Letná Hill used to support a statue of Stalin 20 times life size. When it was blown up in 1962 it was replaced by a giant red metronome marking the progress of time and history.

At the opposite end of the avenue, on the edge of the Old Town Square, **St. Nicholas Church** (*kostel svatého Mikuláše*) was once owned by the Benedictines; nowadays it is a Hussite establishment. Rich Baroque details embellish the church, a monument to Kilian Dientzenhofer's talents. It is also a great venue for chamber concerts held during summer.

Just around the corner, at the crossing of Maiselova and Kaprová streets, is a modern **bust** of Franz Kafka, attached to the house where he was born in 1883. Next to St. Nicholas Church is an exhibition of his life and works. Kafka is better known in the West than on his home ground. He wrote in German, and his nightmarish novels such as *The Castle* and *The Trial* were not translated into Czech until long after his death in 1924. The official perception of his importance in world literature has usually depended on swings in ideology. The communists banned him in 1948, and again after a thaw in the 1960s, as his ideas about alienation were deemed subversive.

Kafka is buried in the New Jewish Cemetery, but for a more hauntingly evocative experience, visitors should seek out the **Old Jewish Cemetery** (*Starý židovský hřbitov*) (enter from U starého hřbitova). In the shade of the lofty, wearily leaning elder trees sprawls a chaotic jumble of 12,000 ancient gravestones, all askew. Over the centuries, the tombstones were all packed tightly together because, with limited space, the bodies had to be buried several layers deep. The oldest gravestone, belonging to a scholar named Avigdor Karo, is dated 1439, while the newest is dated 1787. The most significant Hebrew inscriptions are explained to visitors during guided tours. Be sure to have a look at the tomb of the celebrated Rabbi Löw. This intriguing 16th-century scholar is remembered as the "father" of the Golem, a legendary artificial man created out of the mud of the Vltava.

East of the cemetery, the oddly named **Old-New Synagogue** (*Staronová synagóga*) was new when compared with Prague's original synagogue, but old in relation to the rest. It is one of half a dozen historic synagogues which constitute the **State Jewish Museum**. A steeply pitched roof with huge Gothic gables of brick highlights this 13th-century structure, which is actually taller than it looks; the floor is only one flight down. High vaulted ceilings cover its twin naves, which are still the scene of religious services. During the 17th and 18th centuries new separate areas were added for women worshippers. A banner here (restored during the 18th century) was presented to the Jews of Prague by Charles IV in 1358.

Across a narrow alley from the entrance to the Old-New Synagogue, the **High Synagogue** (*Vysoká synagóga*) has a collection of Jewish ceremonial textiles. The pink Baroque **Jewish Town Hall** (*Židovská radnice*), abutting the synagogue, is the seat of the Chief Rabbi. The building is capped by a clock tower and, just below it, there is another large clock with Hebrew letters denoting the hours; like Hebrew writing, which goes from right to left, the hands go counterclockwise.

The **Maisel Synagogue** bears the name of the 16th-century mayor of the Jewish ghetto, Mordecai Maisela. A tireless do-gooder for his constituents, Maisel also served Emperor Rudolph II

Time stands still in the Old Jewish Cemetery, though not on the Jewish Town Hall clock.

as minister of finance. Founded in the 16th century as a family synagogue in Renaissance style, the building was then subject to additions and re-modellings in later styles—in this case, 1890s Neo-Gothic. The synagogue is renowned for its exhibition of liturgical silver.

The **Pinkas Synagogue**, on the far side of the cemetery, began as one family's house of worship in the 16th century. Expanded and beautified, it later became the fashionable rival to the Old-New Synagogue. After World War II the interior walls were inscribed with the names of all 77,297 Czech victims of the Nazis.

In the former **Ceremonial Hall** (*Bývalá obřadní síň*), next to the cemetery entrance, is a deeply moving collection of children's art created during their confinement in the Theresienstadt (Terezín) concentration camp in the 1940s. Pictured are scenes of everyday life as well as the children's own dreams. The site of the camp itself, only about 48 km (30 miles) from Prague, can be visited.

More Old Town Monuments

The influential theologian Jan Hus is remembered in the **Bethlehem Chapel** (*Betlémská kaple*), a reconstruction of the original 14th-century hall where he used to preach his revolutionary theses. After Hus was excommunicated and executed, the chapel served as headquarters of the Hussite movement. When the Counter-Reformation won control of Bohemia, it was taken over by the Jesuits. Little of the original building was left by the time it was decided to reconstruct it in the 1950s, but some authentic inscriptions have recently been restored.

The Jesuits were responsible for the great **Clementinum** (*Klementinum*), a complex of buildings so formidable that a whole neighbourhood had to be razed to make room for the project. The dramatic Baroque façade all along Křižovnická Street gives only a hint of its real size. Walk through the courtyards to experience the feeling of immensity of this mini-city, built in the late 17th and early 18th centuries. High above the compound, one of its towers displays the time; the other, the Observatorium, gave a head start to many early 18th-century astronomers. The Clementinum now houses several million books as well as the thousands of rare medieval manuscripts of the National Library of the Czech Republic.

Facing the eastern tower of Charles Bridge, **St. Saviour Church** (*kostel svatého Salvátora*) once belonged to the Clementinum, though it is much older, construction having begun in 1578. The interior is much more inspiring than its grey outer walls might suggest. It was first built in Renaissance style, but was later amended with some effusive Baroque afterthoughts.

On Křižovnické Square, **St. Francis Seraphim church** (*kostel svatého Františka Serafinského*) is the work of the French architect Jean-Baptiste Mathey. A grand cupola sets the style for this stately structure, built between 1679 and 1689. The inside of the dome is the "canvas" for a fresco of the *Last Judgement*.

The Jewish Cemetery is worth a close look.

The majestic **monument** in the middle of the small square features a statue of Emperor Charles IV. It was dedicated in 1848, on the 500th anniversary of Charles University. From here, take a closer look at the Vltava River. Another place of interest in the vicinity is the Smetana Museum (see page 69).

NEW TOWN

Although the vast majority of its medieval monuments have been swept away, Prague's New Town (*Nové Město*) is far older than you may imagine. It was founded by Charles IV in 1348 to ease crowding in the historic core of the city. The district soon became a centre of commerce, where artisans and traders settled and thrived. With its hotels and restaurants, theatres and shops, the New Town is the liveliest part of Prague, and pedestrian zones greatly enhance the pleasure of exploring the area.

Wenceslas Square

More of a gardened boulevard than a broad open plaza, Wenceslas Square (*Václavské náměstí*) is Prague's answer to the Champs-Elysées, though not quite so long or wide or fashionable. Find a seat at one of the outdoor cafés facing the square and enjoy watching all of Prague stroll past.

Hotels, department stores, offices, and cinema complexes line the boulevard, which measures some 60 by 680 meters (197 by 2,230 feet). Almost all the buildings were designed or remodelled in the 20th century; they include some fine examples of Art Nouveau and Constructivist styles.

At the lower end of the square, the street known as **Na příkopě** divides the Old and New towns. Na příkopě, which means On the Moat, was built on top of a medieval moat marking the municipal boundaries. Nowadays, it's the city's busiest pedestrians-only street. The national tourist agency, Čedok, operates from a former bank at number 18; the Prague Information Service is situated at number 20. Some other notable landmarks on this street are: several bank buildings designed in the pompous styles of their eras, a Baroque palace now converted to a club, restaurants, and exclusive shops.

The street parallel to carless Na příkopě, by contrast clamorous with traffic, is Jindřišská ulice, which cuts across the middle of Wenceslas Square. The main **post office** (*pošta*), a 19th-century palace, was actually built on the site of a medieval botanical garden. At the far end of the street stands one of the New Town's oldest survivors, **St. Henry's church** (*kostel svatého Jindřicha*). Established in 1348, the interior now contains several remarkable 18th-century altarpieces.

At the top end of Wenceslas Square crowds naturally gravitate towards one of Prague's favourite symbols: the

Not exactly a square, Prague's answer to the Champs-Elysées is a popular meeting place and busy commercial centre.

equestrian **statue** of the martyr St. Wenceslas. This 20th-century monument to the tenth-century prince is by the Czech sculptor Josef Václav Myslbek. Guarding the corners of the pedestal are four other patron saints of Bohemia: Procopius, Agnes, Adalbert, and Ludmilla.

Near the statue is a plaque, which marks the spot where a young student of philosophy burned himself alive in 1969 in protest of the Soviet invasion. The shrine to Jan Palach which was formed here during the momentous events of November 1989 has been turned into a permanent memorial for the victims of communism.

Behind the monument to St. Wenceslas, across the noisy avenue (Mezibranská), is a vast Neo-Renaissance palace, with a great central dome and other heroic touches. It has the look of a national capitol building, but actually serves as the **National Museum** (*Národní muzeum*), a role for which it was built at the end of the 19th century. The earth below the museum is now honeycombed with tunnels which connect two Metro lines and offer pedestrian routes to the nearby streets and buildings, free of traffic and weather hazards.

Two other buildings stand out along the same avenue, which is the main north–south thoroughfare. The **State Opera** (formally the Smetana Theatre) (*Smetanovo divadlo*), designed originally as a venue for German-language operas, is a Neo-Classical building reconstructed in recent times. It now specializes mainly in Czech operas. The theatre is not to be confused with Smetana Hall, the main concert site in the Prague Communal Building, or, for that matter, the Smetana Museum, which is right alongside Charles Bridge. Prague is clearly proud of the great composer, who, like Beethoven, wrote some of his most memorable music after going deaf.

The **Main Rail Station** (*Hlavní nádraží*) is more than just a place to catch a train. A very grand example of Art Nouveau style, it dates from the first decade of the 20th century. Inside, the upper level retains many sumptuous features which celebrate the self-confidence of the age.

Half-way down the square, at numbers 25 to 27, the **Grand Hotel Evropa** is a glorious example of Art Nouveau indulgence. The café terrace on the outside provides a good view of the passing crowds, but it is the interior which really impresses.

A short walk away, among the luxurious old buildings of Hybernská Street, the most pampered is the Kinský Palace. Built in Baroque style in the 17th century, it was remodelled more than a century later. The building became the property of the Social Democratic Party in 1907 and was known as The People's House. In 1912 a conference of the Russian Social Democratic Party took place here, chaired by Lenin. It now houses the American Cultural Centre.

The Polished Polka

Bedřich Smetana (1824–1884), father of the Czech school of composition, put the polka into classical music. In *The Bartered Bride,* his most successful opera, he gave new prestige to this vivacious peasant dance. In spite of its name, the polka (meaning Polish girl) is strictly a Czech invention. Legend says it was first improvised by a Bohemian peasant girl around 1830. Within a decade, the rage of Prague was being danced all over Europe, a double-time rival to the waltz.

Another Czech composer who "borrowed" the polka, Antonín Dvořák (1841–1904), became internationally renowned for his operas, symphonies, a requiem, and *Slavonic Dances*. Early in his career Dvořák was a violinist in Prague's National Theatre orchestra, conducted by Maestro Smetana.

Finally, **U Hybernů House** (*dům U hybernů*), which faces Republic Square (*Náměstí republiky*), is a haughty example of Empire style. U Hybernů (which means At the Hibernians) was the site of a Franciscan monastery built in the 17th century by monks who came over from Ireland.

West of Wenceslas Square

Lost in a monastery complex in the middle of the city, the immensely tall and narrow **church of Our Lady of the Snows** (*chrám Panny Marie Sněžné*) was actually founded by Charles IV in the 14th century. Despite its impressive dimensions, it never reached the full size of the original Gothic blueprint. A mosaic of *Virgin and Child* on the south façade recalls the art of Byzantine churches; inside, there is a splendid Baroque altar. This church was a hotbed of the Hussite movement in the 15th century, when the fiery Hussite priest Jan Želivský preached here. He was the leader of the 1419 raid on the New Town Hall in which rebels jettisoned city councillors, the first of Prague's famous defenestrations. The Franciscan abbey adjoining the church has a delightful wine cellar and an attractive park.

> On timetables, train trips requiring reservations are marked with an R in a box when it is essential, and in a circle when advisable.

From here down to the river, **National Avenue** (*Národní třída*) has been a key artery for more than two centuries. Like Na příkopě, this street dividing the Old and New towns follows the course of a moat. A mixed assortment of buildings lines the avenue, from extravagant Baroque palaces to box-like modern glass houses. The biggest of these is the K-Mart Department Store.

National Avenue's most monumental building is the **National Theatre** (*Národní divadlo*), another Neo-Renaissance creation of the late 19th century. The architect, Josef Zítek, a professor at Prague Technical University, had to cope with a smallish, irregular site, but managed to squeeze everything in, to the admiration of most of the citizens. One month before the official opening night in 1881 the roof caught fire, theatrically destroying everything except the walls; the city's firemen, who all happened to be attending a funeral, failed to turn up. In the rebuilding, the number of seats was reduced, the number of fire escapes increased. The theatre was again lavishly restored in the 1970s and 1980s.

Nová scéna (The New Stage), the modern addition alongside the nation's paramount opera house, has a surprising façade of glass bricks. The theatre, initially designed for chamber works, seats several hundred people.

If Wenceslas Square is far more a boulevard than a plaza, then **Charles Square** (*Karlovo náměstí*) is more a park. Prague's biggest square, laid out in 1348, used to be a livestock and vegetable market until it was refurbished in the middle part of the 19th century. The park is now speckled with fountains and statues.

The historic building from which Father Želivský and his co-conspirators defenestrated several municipal officials was the **New Town Hall** (*Novoměstská radnice*), on the north side of the square. The Hussite raiders also liberated some of their cohorts from the prison on the premises. Now, very little of the original 14th-century building remains after a series of reconstruction projects over many centuries.

Art Nouveau décor on Prague's magnificent Municipal House in Republic Square.

In Resslova Street, to the west of the square, the Baroque **church of Saints Cyril and Methodius** (*kostel svatého Cyrila a Metoděje*), dedicated to the ninth-century monks who first brought Christianity to the Slavs, is the Orthodox cathedral of Prague. Note the bullet holes in the wall around the crypt window. In 1942 six Czech resistance fighters who had parachuted in from Britain died here during a German assault on their hiding place. The team was responsible for assassinating Prague's Nazi overlord, Reinhard Heydrich, nicknamed "the Hangman." Before the siege of the church, the SS had already avenged Heydrich's death by, among other things, obliterating the village of Lidice (see page 77).

On the east side of Charles Square, the attractively situated **St. Ignatius church** (*kostel svatého Ignáce*) was built as a Jesuit stronghold in 1699. The elaborate gold-leaf decoration verges on the Rococo.

Facing Charles Square from the south, **Faust House** (*Faustův dům*) got its name from the 16th-century legend examined in Goethe's haunting drama. The connection is as

---

The War Švejk Lost

Jaroslav Hasek was less than 40 years old when he died in 1923, leaving behind an unfinished masterpiece. His book, *The Good Soldier Svejk*, is the riotous saga of a wily warrior, "certified feebleminded," who always succeeds in wearing down the bureaucracy. It has inspired generations of pacifists and downtrodden ordinary people caught in the throes of 20th-century life. Only a few books have so effectively undermined the myths surrounding the heroics of warfare.

Hasek wrote from personal experience. He served in the Austrian army during World War I and was taken prisoner by the Russians. Another similarity to his fictional hero: Hašek sometimes earned money peddling dogs with bogus pedigrees. Then came the disillusionment of the dogs of war.

vague as this: the house was once occupied by alchemists, and the neighbours suspected their experiments of involving devilishly strange goings-on, even spreading the wild rumour that Dr. Faust sold his soul to the devil under this very roof. The building itself was designed as a Renaissance mansion, but later turned Baroque.

A pair of startlingly modern white spires, resembling two rockets frozen in the sky a few seconds after blast-off, mark the former **Emmaus Abbey** (*klášter na Slovanech*). The pinnacles provided a solution to the problem created by American pilots late in World War II when they bombed the 14th-century church. In its early years this Benedictine monastery aimed to attract those Slavs hitherto devoted to the Orthodox faith, and so the Catholic mass here was said in Church Slavonic rather than in Latin. There are fine, though heavily restored, 14th-century frescoes in the cloister.

Across Vyšehradská Street from the monastery a lovely Baroque church is set on a bluff. Its name is a mouthful: The **church of St. John of Nepomuk on the Rock** (*kostel svatého Jana Nepomuckého na skálce*). The architect Kilian Dientzenhofer, who designed this church, was also the author of the most inspired Baroque church in Prague, St. Nicholas in the Lesser Quarter (see page 39). Here he overcame the problem of a steep, narrow site with a high-flying church of theatrical symmetry.

Dientzenhofer also gained credit for **Villa Amerika,** a delightful mansion in a little park of its own in Ke Karlovu Street. The American connection is indirect: apparently there used to be an inn nearby named "America." The building now serves as the **Antonín Dvořák Museum.** By coincidence, Dvořák spent several years in the United States, where he composed his *From the New World* symphony.

Around the corner in Na bojišti Street, a tavern called **U kalicha** (The Chalice) is usually packed with tourists who have come to eat pork ribs and dumplings, drink beer, and pay tribute to a sort of war hero. In this beer hall the quintessential Czech hero, the fictional Good Soldier Švejk, whiled away many a happy hour before "intervening" in World War I. In reality, Švejk's creator, Jaroslav Hašek, was a regular hero.

Vyšehrad

As in the days of the mystical Princess Libuše, who foresaw Prague's greatness many centuries ago, there is a choice view over the Vltava from the cliff's edge at Vyšehrad. In spite of its legendary connection with the princess, the right-bank fortress is probably only the second-oldest part of the city. In the 11th century, King Vratislav II moved here from the earliest Prague Castle, Hradčany. Then, less than a century later, the court was transferred back across the river. Even so, Vyšehrad (High Castle) retained at least ceremonial importance: Charles IV insisted that long coronation processions through the whole city and up the hill to Prague Castle should start here. The present fortress walls were begun during the reign of King Charles IV. A century later, the area suffered devastation during the Hussite wars, and its character changed. From being closely linked with the monarchy, it became a "free town" of traders and craftspeople. Not much of irresistible interest remains, except for an ancient chapel, a celebrated cemetery, and a Neo-Gothic church.

The oldest building of Vyšehrad, **St. Martin's Rotunda** (*rotunda svatého Martina*), is a Romanesque round chapel of the 11th century. Like quite a few of the venerable buildings in Prague, it suffered many of the indignities of history. Somewhere along the line military priorities transcended religious needs, and the chapel was turned into a gunpowder magazine.

But its architectural importance was rediscovered late on in the 19th century, and the rotunda was restored.

The little **church of Saints Peter and Paul** (*kostel sv. Petra a Pavla*) looks as old as the Middle Ages, but its landmark towers are 20th-century versions of Gothic style. Mosaics on the façade give it an Eastern quality. Outstanding among the works of art inside, a Gothic painting of the Virgin dates from the 14th century.

The thought of visiting a cemetery may leave you cold, but the **National Cemetery** (*Vyšehradský hřbitov*), next to the church, is not an ordinary graveyard. Some of its tombs are the necropolitan equivalent of the mansions that the rich burghers enjoyed in life. Look over the sculptural effusions, the Art Nouveau design, the floral offerings and the names, which are a roll of honour of some leading Czech citizens, including Neruda, Aleš, Dvořák, and Smetana.

Over the Bridge

A lot of water has flowed under the bridge since Charles IV built his sturdy span across the Vltava. A number of newer bridges now stand shoulder to shoulder along the river, but Prague's most original modern bridge crosses no river. The **Nuselský most** strides efficiently across the popu-

Eleventh-century St. Martin's Rotunda has survived the passage of time.

lous Nusle Valley. A six-lane highway occupies the top level
of the bridge, which is 500 meters (1,640 feet) long, while in
its streamlined underbelly runs a Metro line. Passengers who
feel deprived of the scenery get their reward at the Vyšehrad
Metro station, which is above ground and all view.

The Metro station leads to the **Prague Palace of Culture**
(*Palác kultury Praha*), the capital's prime venue for events
such as political rallies, concerts, and the international book
fair in May. The main Congress Hall seats over 2,800, and
there are smaller halls for other functions. The building is
equipped with the most up-to-date computer systems.

Across the highway, you'll see a modern skyscraper hotel,
the **Hotel Forum Praha,** which has over 500 guest rooms
and a conference centre. Among the usual five-star facilities,
the hotel plays host to Prague's first gambling casino.

MUSEUMS

Prague's museums concentrate on themes as broad as literature or as specialized as the life and work of a single composer. As for art, galleries show to good advantage an
unsuspected wealth of old masters, even older masters, and
modern works as well. The following is a brief review of
the city's principal museums. As a general rule, opening
times are 10:00 A.M. to 6:00 P.M. from Tuesday to Sunday;
most museums close on Monday, except the State Jewish
Museum, which keeps the Sabbath.

In a Neo-Renaissance palace backing on to the old Prague
ghetto, the **Museum of Decorative Arts** (*Uměleckoprůmyslové muzeum*) at 17. listopadu 2, Prague 1, highlights the
craftsmanship of old and modern masters of Czech crystal,
porcelain, and woodcarving. Confirming the importance of
beer in local society, there are some huge illustrated beer
mugs from the 16th and 17th centuries. You can also see the

domestic and foreign achievements in clock-making, cabi-net-making, and bookbinding.

Bertramka is the name of the villa where Mozart lived on various occasions in the late 18th century. In a wooded estate near the peaceful Malá Strana cemetery, the little museum displays historic scores and letters, and musical instruments. The street address, appropriately, is Mozartova 169, Prague 5. The museum is open daily from 9:30 A.M. to 6:00 P.M., with indoor concerts at 5:00 P.M. Thursday to Saturday.

The **Prague City Museum** (*Muzeum hlavního města Prahy*), next to the Florence Metro station, presents the city's turbulent history in an uncluttered, graphic style. The centre of attraction upstairs is a remarkably complex, homemade

Riverside vistas delight the eye and bring an air of tranquillity to the bustle of cental Prague.

papier-mâché model of the city of Prague as it looked during the early 19th century. Opening times are from 9:00 A.M. to 6:00 P.M., closed Mondays.

The **Muzeum Antonína Dvořáka** in Villa Amerika, a small, red palace at Ke Karlovu 20, Prague 2, honours the Czech Republic's best-known composer. Antonín Dvořák (1841–1904) was widely honoured in his lifetime, as is well documented here. You can see the cap and gown that he wore when he received an honorary doctorate from Cambridge University in 1891. On show, too, are his original scores, quill, and other belongings, and souvenirs of the time he lived in the town of Spillville, Iowa.

The **Náprstek Museum** (*Náprstkovo muzeum*) was founded in 1862 by Vojta Náprstek, a representative of the Czech bourgeoisie. Today the building on Betlémské Square houses a collection of artefacts from Amerindian, Australian, African, and Asian cultures which is part of the National Museum collection.

The **State Jewish Museum** (*Státní židovské muzeum*) has its own version of a diaspora. The exhibits (closed Saturdays and Jewish religious holidays) are distributed among several buildings in the Josefov quarter, including six historic synagogues. The Klaus Synagogue contains documentation on the arts and religious practices of Prague's ancient Jewish community. The best of the exhibits were gathered during World War II, when the Nazis searched out every last ethnological detail about a people they planned to eliminate.

Next to the Lesser Quarter Square in former Michna Palace is the **Museum of Physical Culture and Sport,** with a permanent exhibition featuring "The Glory of Sport."

Historic Strahov Monastery, southwest of Hradčany, is the striking setting for the **National Literature Memorial** (*Památník národního písemnictví*). Book lovers, whether or

MUSEUM AND GALLERY HIGHLIGHTS

Before you plan your visit, it's wise to check precise opening times at the tourist information office or in the bi-weekly English-language publication *Prognosis*. Czech names are given in brackets.

Museum of Czech Music: Ke Karlovu 20, Prague 2; 10am–5pm daily except Monday; Metro C: I. P. Pavlova. Memorable music in fabulous Baroque villa devoted to the life and works of the Czech composer Antonín Dvořák. (See page 65)

Bertramka: Mozartova 169, Prague 5; 9:30am–6pm daily, indoor concerts at 5pm Thursday, Friday, and Saturday; trams 4, 6, 7, 9. Mozartian memorabilia in a delightful setting in the leafy suburbs of Prague. (See page 64)

Collection of Old Bohemian Art (*Sbírka starého českého umění*): St. George's Convent, Jiřské náměstí 33, Prague Castle; 10am–6pm Tuesday to Sunday, closed Monday; Metro A: Hradčanská; tram 22 to Pražský hrad. The National Gallery's treasured Baroque paintings in a 1000-year-old former convent. (See page 68)

Museum of Decorative Arts (*Uměleckoprůmyslové muzeum*): 17 listopadu 2, Prague 1; 10am–6pm daily except Monday; trams 17, 18. Displays of Czech crystal and porcelain. (See page 63)

National Gallery European Collection, Sternberg Palace (*Šternberský Palác/Národní galerie*): Hradčanské náměstí 15; 10am–6pm daily except Monday; tram 22. Excellent collection of European art, from Cranach and Brueghel to Picasso and Braque. (See opposite page)

National Technical Museum (*Národní technické muzeum*): Kostelní 42, Prague 7; 9am–5pm daily except Monday; walk up Kostelní towards the Letná Plain. Fascinating collection of historical technological achievements. (See page 69)

St. Agnes's Convent (*Klášter sv. Anežsky*): Anežská, on the corner of U milosrdných; 10am–6pm daily except Monday; trams 5, 14, 26; bus 125. The National Gallery's collection of modern Czech painting. (See page 69)

State Jewish Museum (*Státní židovské muzeum*): Jáchymova 3, Prague 1; 9am–5pm (last entry 4:30) daily except Saturdays and Jewish holidays; Metro A: Staroměstská. Exhibits documenting Prague's Jewish community in historic synagogues. (See page 65) not they understand Czech, will appreciate the museum's display of precious old books and manuscripts—illuminated psalters, hymnals, and scientific treatises. There are also sculptures and historical maps, theatre bills and cartoons. The anteroom to the Philosophical Hall has a few curiosities on display: cases containing seashells and butterflies constitute an early-18th-century prototype of a museum.

The striking Renaissance Schwarzenberg Palace, just outside the walls of Prague Castle, now serves as command post and parade ground of the **Military History Museum** (*Vojenské historické muzeum*). Considered one of the most comprehensive of its kind in the world, the collection starts with an axe head from around 3000 B.C. and works its way through the evolution of weaponry to the 20th-century cannon. Also on show are guns and banners from the French Revolution of 1789.

At the top end of Wenceslas Square, the building of the **National Museum** (*Národní muzeum*) sums up the adjective "palatial." It's a good place to remember on a Monday, which is when almost all the other museums in Prague are closed. The historical, archaeological, and numismatic collections are situated here, and a Pantheon holds statues of the nation's illustrious progeny. Under the same roof is the Museum of Natural Sciences, a collection of animal, vegetable, and mineral specimens.

The principal building of the **National Gallery** (*Národní galerie*) is the for-

The National Gallery, a former convent, houses a priceless collection of Baroque paintings.

mer Sternberg Palace, virtually hidden away behind the Archbishop's Palace at Hradčanské náměstí 15, just outside the walls of Prague Castle. Don't be discouraged by the roundabout entranceway that looks as if you may be using the servants' door; just follow the signs. The Collection of Old European Art, from the 14th to the 18th centuries, excludes Bohemian artists, who rate their own museum. Outstanding here are the Italian Renaissance paintings, Byzantine and Russian icons, and rare German and Flemish works. Among the best known painters represented are three dynasties: the Brueghels, the Cranachs, and the Holbeins. A position of honour is given to Dürer's *Madonna of the Rose Garlands* (1506), considered the first group portrait in German art.

For the National Gallery's Modern and Contemporary Art collection, visit **Veletrzni Palace**, at Dukelskych hrdinu 47, Prague 7. Highlights include 19th- and 20th-century French painting featuring several Impressionist greats; works by Picasso and Braque are also on display.

The National Gallery's superb **Collection of Old Bohemian Art** (*Sbírka starého çeského umění*) fills all three floors of the thousand-year-old former Convent of St. George, inside Prague Castle. Among hundreds of works, largely on religious themes, the most extraordinary are a

Ornate ceiling frescoes in the Strahor Monastery library merit close study.

set of icons from Karlstejn Castle by Master Theodoric. Among Czech Baroque painters, it is well worth discovering the portraits by Karel Skréta, Jan Kupecky, and Anthony Kern.

In a far-flung corner of the Old Town, the Convent of the Blessed Agnes (*Ane.sky kláster*) is now the distinguished Gothic home of the National Gallery's **Collection of Modern Czech Painting.** The pictures on show chart the progress of Czech art from Romanticism to Symbolism.

In the Second Courtyard of the castle, the **Prague Castle Picture Gallery** (*Obrazárna Pra.ského hradu*) displays a few dozen outstanding paintings by Old Masters. The collection was begun in the 16th century by the reclusive art lover Rudolph II, the emperor who moved his capital from Vienna to Prague. A majority of these paintings were carried off as war booty in 1648; you will have to go to Stockholm to see them. Of special interest here are works by Tintoretto, Rubens, and Veronese. The gallery's opening times can be erratic, so check beforehand.

The **Smetana Museum** (*Muzeum Bedricha Smetany*) Novotného lávka 1, Prague 1, dedicated to the life and works of Bedrich Smetana, will probably appeal only to serious fans of the composer. Most of the displays consist of family photos, original scores, and some newspaper reviews in Czech. But the situation, on a mini-peninsula by the side of Charles Bridge, and the Neo-Renaissance building are perfect. It is open Wednesday to Monday, 10:00 A.M. to 5:00 P.M.

Prague's **National Technical Museum** (*Národní technické muzeum*), housed in a 1930s building and out of the way at Kostelní 42, Prague 7, contains thousands of fascinating utilitarian objects. The exhibits include a collection of vintage cars, a royal railway carriage used by the Habsburgs, and a dozen old aeroplanes suspended in mid-air.

See the *Prague Post* for details of temporary exhibitions.

EXCURSIONS

Organized day trips from Prague reveal the grandeur of Czech castles, which come in all models, from stark Gothic fortresses to Baroque pleasure palaces. Other highlights are historic towns and famous spa resorts. Along the way to these cultural rendezvous, relish the restful scenery of Bohemia's fields and forests.

There are many fascinating places which can be visited in a day. Here are some suggestions, in alphabetical order, for excursion stops within easy distance of Prague.

České Budějovice

A scenic drive through typical villages will take you to the delightful and historic town of České Budějovice, the regional capital of South Bohemia and home of the famed Budvar (Budweiser) beer. Situated almost 140 km (87 miles) south of Prague, this town was established in the 13th century by King Otakar II. The medieval central square, reputedly the largest in the world, is lined with impressive Baroque and Renaissance houses. Although some of the streets off the main square have a dishevelled air in comparison with Prague's fresh and brightly painted exteriors, the old area around the Gothic church is well worth exploring.

Beer has been brewed in České Budějovice since the early 16th century. A perfect place to sample the local tipple is Masné Krámy, a historic and popular beer arcade situated just off the main square.

 ## Hluboká Castle

Renovation in the 19th century converted this ancient fortress into a crenellated construction like a child's toy castle. You half expect to see it guarded by miniature soldiers in bearskin hats. The decorations tend toward the overwhelming; keeping track of the ceilings alone is a major undertaking.

North of České Budějovice, Hluboká Castle dominates the Vltava River. Its dramatic history begins in the middle of the 13th century. One of the castle's early owners, Záviš of Falknštejn, lost a great political struggle, the property, and his life: in 1290 he was executed in a meadow in the shadow of the castle. After some interim digressions the castle came into the Holy Roman hands of King Charles IV.

In the 16th century the original Gothic castle was converted into a Renaissance château. When the Baroque craze came in a while later, the place was rebuilt. The owners were the Schwarzenberg family, German nobles who prospered in the service of the Habsburg dynasty. They soon acquired more property than any other landlords in Bohemia, holding on to it until nationalization after World War II.

The final improvements for Hluboká Castle, begun under Johann Adolf II of Schwarzenberg in the mid-19th century, were inspired by the Gothic style. To enhance the romantic effect, an unusually spacious English garden was created.

On the way into the complex, notice a hunting motif as subtle as a blast from a blunderbuss: sculpted deers' heads project from the walls in the courtyard, but the antlers are real. Among the castle's collections are medieval weapons and knights' armour. Also here are precious Flemish tapestries and antique furniture.

Finally, the former stables contain a worthy collection of Bohemian art, most of which are medieval religious works. The castle can be visited between April and October.

Karlovy Vary

Owing to its handsome site and curative mineral springs, Karlovy Vary, situated 130 km (80 miles) west of the capital, has attracted a most illustrious crowd of health faddists down through the centuries. To drop a few historical names: Bach, Goethe, Gogol, Liszt, Brahms, and Grieg all came here to enjoy the spas, as did political figures Czar Peter the Great and Karl Marx.

Gone, alas, is the glamour of pre-war days. Most of the curists sucking hot water from their special spouted cups look glumly ill or convalescent, socially a long way from the old crowd of crowned heads, nabobs, and snobs. Still, the stately spa town, hidden in a ring of richly wooded hills, is a pleasant outing in nostalgia.

Karlovy Vary (known formerly as Karlsbad) is named after Charles IV, who put his imperial seal of approval on the spa in the 14th century. Members of his hunting party, rushing after a deer, are said to have discovered the first hot spring, and medieval medicine men were soon prescribing the waters for many ailments. The early patients had to spend hours every day bathing in the hot springs, as well as bloating them-

The many bridges that span Karlovy River are as useful as they are picturesque.

selves by consuming the health-giving water. The treatment nowadays is much more selective and less draconian.

Proceeding from fountain to fountain (walking is as important as drinking), people taking the cure can admire the town's architectural landmarks. The **church of Mary Magdalene** (*kostel Maří Magdalény*) was designed in the 1730s by Kilian Dientzenhofer of Prague Baroque fame. The filigreed wooden **Market Colonnade** has been eclipsed by the Neo-Classical-style **Mill Colonnade** (built by the Czech architect Josef Zítek). The newest attraction for the mineral-water version of a pub-crawl is the modern **Spring Colonnade,** with a geyser wheezing, spitting, and exploding in its own rotunda. Here the taps flow with water from various local sources, at natural temperatures as hot as 72°C (162°F). Generally it tastes either rusty or unexceptional—not everybody's cup of tea.

As in the great old days of Karlsbad, the balneological equivalent of après-ski activities are supposed to be as stimulating as the treatments. Karlovy Vary has an international film festival, concerts and theatrical programmes, an art gallery, and many cafés and restaurants. Shoppers can dabble in porcelain and glassware, the local liqueur (called the "13th curative spring"), and the highly prized wafers (*oplátky*) of Karlovy Vary, which taste like virgin ice-cream cones.

Karlštejn Castle

The Holy Roman Emperor Charles IV, who transformed Prague into a capital of European culture, built this classic castle to protect the crown jewels behind walls 6 meters (20 feet) thick. For added security he chose a sheer hilltop site in the pine-forest country 28 km (17 miles) southwest of Prague. Hrad (castle) Karlštejn, the most visited monument beyond the city limits, is everybody's idea of a medieval castle.

Imposing Karlštejn Castle: Charles IV chose a hilltop site to safeguard the crown jewels.

In spite of its impregnable air Karlštejn developed a certain vulnerability. It survived a protracted siege by powerfully armed Hussite rebels in 1422 with less than flying colours. Again, in a footnote to the Thirty Years' War, Swedish attackers gravely damaged the castle in 1648; Charles IV could not have anticipated the power of modern field artillery which the Swedes pioneered. A serious restoration project finally got under way late in the 19th century.

Inside the **Imperial Palace** (*Císařský palác*), one of the many imposing buildings behind the crenellated walls, there are exhibitions largely devoted to the life and times of the founding emperor. In the king's audience hall, the original wood panelling of the walls and ceilings has been restored. In an early example of royal one-upmanship, the throne was positioned in such a way as to let glaring sunlight intimidate visitors who dared to try to look the monarch in the eye. Luxembourg Hall contains an intricate tapestry version of the family tree of the house of Luxembourg.

Some precious Gothic wall paintings have been discovered in the **church of Our Lady**, including scenes featuring Charles himself. Connected to this small church is a much smaller **chapel of St. Catherine,** the emperor's own private retreat, its walls studded with semi-precious stones.

In the castle keep, the **Holy Cross chapel** (*Kaple svatého Kříže*) was once the repository of the crown jewels and other regalia. Behind the altar, too, the most vital state documents were well preserved. The state treasures were symbolically guarded by a "heavenly army" of more than 100 saints as portrayed in remarkable paintings by the 14th-century court artist, Master Theodoric. His technique was centuries ahead of his time. (The originals are now displayed in the National Gallery's Collection of Old Bohemian Art in Prague.) The newly renovated chapel is well worth a visit.

Konopiště Castle

Like Karlštejn, the castle of Konopiště began as a bristling Gothic fortress. But this lion ended up as a lamb: a hunting lodge for the ill-fated heir to the Habsburg throne.

Situated some 44 km (27 miles) southwest of Prague, Konopiště was built in the late 13th century in the style of a French fortress. The layout made it all but unbeatable as a redoubt. By the 17th century, the Swedish army showed how warfare had changed, and the castle of Konopiště fell.

Early in the 18th century the Count of Vrtba bought the place and began revolutionary renovations. In the vulnerable castle's new peaceful mode, Konopiště became the Baroque country home of a well-to-do family. In 1887, however, the property was taken over by the Austrian Archduke Franz Ferdinand, who greatly expanded and improved the building.

Franz Ferdinand was noted for his great love of hunting. He was, in truth, a fanatic. He gunned down almost anything with four feet or two wings. Thousands of his own trophies cover the walls of this ostentatious lodge. Franz Ferdinand also collected armour. The splendid display at Konopiště is as varied and impressive as you'll find in any European castle. It includes some gorgeous horse-and-rider armour for ceremonial jousts, and anything a knight might need, from pikes to mini-cannon.

> **Beer consumption in Czechoslovakia is among the highest in the world.**

The archduke met his destiny at the other end of a gun. His assassination at Sarajevo in 1914 precipitated World War I. During World War II the castle was requisitioned by SS troops, and so many Konopiště treasures found their way to Germany; all have since been recovered.

☛ Kutná Hora

As in Tombstone, Arizona, and Taxco, Mexico, the Czech town of Kutná Hora was built on silver. Founded in the 13th century, when apparently inexhaustible silver deposits were discovered nearby, Kutná Hora soon experienced the joys and growing pains of a boom town. Situated approximately 65 km (40 miles) southeast of the capital, it became the country's second-most-important town in the Middle Ages.

On a bluff overlooking the town, **St. Barbara cathedral** (*chrám sv. Barbory*) looks as if it is about to soar heavenwards, buttresses, spires, and all. Its High Gothic lines were designed in the 14th century; construction went on until the 16th century. The sheer extravagance of the architecture and furnishings testifies to the glorious heyday of this town. The church is dedicated to the patron saint of miners and was financed solely by miners' contributions. A set of frescoes in the cathedral shows miners and minters at work.

The façade of the oldest house in town, referred to as the **Stone House** (*Kamenný dům*), is adorned with exuberant stonework and an inspired oriel window. Another fine relic is the decorative 15th-century town well. Nobody is allowed to tamper with the appearance of the historic centre of Kutná Hora, with its Gothic and Baroque buildings.

The **Italian Court** (the Czech name is *Vlašský dvůr*) was a project of King Wenceslas II. Here, from the very beginning of the 14th century, the local silver was processed into Prague *groschen*, coins that were recognized as legal tender all over Central Europe. The Italian element in the name refers to those skilled minters who were recruited to start production; Florentine bankers soon followed. So did French technicians, specialists in silver casting and minting. The bottom dropped out of the silver business here in 1726, when the mint closed down for lack of raw materials. The most opulent part of the building is the Assembly Hall, with a splendid medieval ceiling.

Lidice

The pilgrimage to Lidice, only 22 km (14 miles) northwest of Prague, serves as a profoundly painful history lesson, and the town remains a tragic monument of resistance to fascism.

Lidice was a small, undistinguished Czech mining village until 1942, when Hitler gave orders for it to be "liquidated" to discourage further resistance. Wiping Lidice off the map—figuratively as well as cartographically—was a well-publicized reprisal for the assassination of SS-Obergruppenführer Reinhard Heydrich. Gestapo and SS troops rounded up the inhabitants, about 450 in all, and burned down every house. They shot all the men (and a few women), then sent the remaining women and some of the children to concentration camps, and handed over other, racially acceptable children for adoption by German families. The village was subsequently flattened and totally removed from sight.

A peaceful green hillside marks the place where the village stood, with a clump of cedars shading the mass

The Lidice memorial is a reminder of the losses incurred during World War II.

grave. Overlooking the site is a small museum containing photos of the victims and mementoes such as bullet-riddled identity cards. The display is simple yet disturbingly effective.

Mariánské Lázně

Like Karlovy Vary, Mariánské Lázně is a spa with a romantic history, occupying a delightful site on a densely wooded hillside. Cultural celebrities such as Goethe, Turgenev, Kafka, Ibsen, and Wagner gravitated to Marienbad, as it was then known, to soak up the beneficial waters as well as inspiration. Goethe fell in love on the spot, prompting him to write *Marienbader Elegie*.

In the far west of the Czech Republic, just across the border from Germany, Mariánské Lázně is founded on water—bubbling mineral springs—but the ozone-rich air is also said to be exceptionally healthful. There are well over a hundred local springs, 40 of which have been credited with therapeutic value. Patients are supposed to spend three weeks in this landscaped array of 19th-century baths and sanatoria. The cure involves drinking oceans of water, bathing in it, and walking at length through the gardens and the forests beyond. There are also mud-baths and injections of carbonic gas bottled at the springs.

By way of a counterpoint to the serious business of health, wholesome distractions are encouraged. The intellectual tone of the old days is maintained with events such as an international music festival and theatrical presentations. Less highbrow are the golf competitions and fashion shows.

Mělník

The hill town of Mělník stands atop the vineyards descending to the strategic junction of the Elbe (*Labe*) and Vltava rivers, some 32 km (20 miles) north of Prague. (Pointing to the relative size of the rivers at this peaceful spot, the locals claim that the Elbe is a tributary of the Vltava and not vice versa, as geography books state.)

Mělník has been a centre of viniculture for more than a millennium. Its quiet, unspoilt town square is a far cry from the bustle of Prague, but the landscape looking down past sloping vineyards at the rivers below is breathtaking.

Legend says the ninth-century Princess Ludmilla originated the idea of using these lands for wine. Charles IV added expertise, importing vines from Burgundy. In spite of this long history, the wines of Mělník are virtually unknown abroad. That's no reason to turn down a tasting in a cool cellar or a cheerful tavern, or both.

The grandest local landmark is **Mělník Castle** (*hrad*). This Renaissance structure houses a truly delightful *vinárna* (wine restaurant), where visitors can now sample the local wine.

Slapy Dam

By car, bus, and boat, holidaymakers (vacationers) from Prague go south to relax at Slapy Dam, on the Vltava River. It's also a customary stop on excursions to nearby Konopiště Castle.

Building this dam, which took four years, changed the look of the surrounding countryside completely. The dam created an artificial lake 40 km (25 miles) long. The woods around the lake provide the pleasant sylvan setting for holiday bungalows and resort colonies, while the waters of the Vltava offer ample opportunity for many recreational pursuits, including swimming, boating, and fishing.

Tábor

On the edge of the town of Tábor, 88 km (55 miles) south of Prague, is an artificial lake called Jordan which is said to date back to the historically eloquent year of 1492. The Hussites used Lake Jordan for baptismal purposes, hence the biblical name. Tábor itself is named after Mount Tabor in Galilee, the biblical scene of a great Israelite victory over the Canaanites, circa 11th century B.C.

The Hussites, members of a religious and political reform movement, split into two factions early in the 15th century. The more militant ones were called Taborites, referring to the town they made their headquarters. Tábor was very well fortified in anticipation of an attack by anti-reformist crusaders of the Holy Roman Empire; the streets of the old town are still laid out in a maze to make the way more difficult for invaders.

The **town square,** Žižkovo náměstí, honours Jan Žižka, the Hussite military chief, who was based here. This splendid, spacious square looks eminently peaceful, but tunnels and cellars were dug beneath it for use in a siege. The Gothic **town hall** is largely dedicated to a museum of the Hussite movement, with considerable documentation about Žižka, the one-eyed military genius. (But different representations fail to agree as to which eye was covered with a patch.) The most remarkable aspect of the town hall from an architectural perspective is its vast ceremonial chamber, which is unmarred by the supporting columns. It may very well be the mightiest non-royal, non-ecclesiastical hall of its era.

Follow the Signs

Here are some key words to help you around Prague:

hrad	castle	*nábřeži*	embankment
kaple	chapel	*náměstí*	square
kostel	church	*palác*	palace
klášter	convent, monastery	*památník*	monument
mešto	town, city	*ulice*	street
most	bridge	*věž*	tower
muzeum	museum	*zahrada*	garden

PRAGUE HIGHLIGHTS

For those on a brief visit to Prague or who want to see the main sights before making a more comprehensive tour of the city, here are the principal highlights, in no order of priority. Czech names are given in brackets.

Charles Bridge (*Karlův most*): Metro A: Staroměstská. Gothic gateways lead onto a 14th-century bridge adorned with Baroque statues. The oldest bridge in Prague is a work of art—and will delight pedestrians as it's also traffic-free. (See page 34)

Lesser Quarter (*Malá Strana*): Metro A: Malostranská. In the shadow of Prague Castle, Baroque charm enchants in the second oldest part of the city. (See page 34)

Old Jewish Town (*Josefov*): Metro A: Staroměstská; trams 17, 18. A wealth of Jewish history in a corner of Prague. (See page 47)

Old Town Square (*Staroměstské náměstí*): Metro A: Staroměstská. Medieval centre of the city, surrounded by dazzling architectural gems and containing a 15th-century astronomical clock. Arrive on the hour to watch figures emerge as the clock strikes. (See page 41)

Our Lady of Loreto (*Loreta*): Tram 22 to Pohořelec. One of the city's most impressive Baroque churches contains a fabulous treasury of religious artefacts. (See page 26)

Prague Castle (*Pražský hrad*): 5am–midnight, closed Monday; Metro A: Hradčanská; tram 22. An ancient complex of palaces, museums, towers, and churches, including the largely Gothic St. Vitus cathedral, last resting place of St. Wenceslas. Stunning views over the city. (See page 28)

Strahov Monastery (*Strahovský klášter*): Open daily except Monday 9am–noon, 12:30–5pm; tram 22. Superb 17th-century library; a magnificent collection of books, manuscripts, and maps and astonishing 18th-century ceiling frescoes. (See page 33)

Vyšehrad Metro C: Vyšehrad. The legendary foundation site of Prague; the fortress has spectacular views over the river. (See page 61)

Wenceslas Square (*Václavské náměstí*): Metro A: Můstek. This is the bustling commercial centre of Prague, which is dominated by a huge statue of St. Wenceslas. (See page 53)

WHAT TO DO

ENTERTAINMENT

Whether your preferences tend towards the frivolous or more cultural diversions, Prague is very well equipped to entertain you. From discos to grand opera, from cabaret to drama, you'll be exhausted long before you can exhaust the capital's possibilities. For a complete review of the more serious attractions, look for the mini-guide "Welcome to Prague" which lists forthcoming events, issued quarterly in English, French, and German editions by the Prague Information Service. It's free at hotels or information offices.

Music has always been one of Prague's strong points ever since Mozart and Beethoven used to captivate the local audiences. (So did Berlioz, Liszt, Tchaikovsky, and Wagner.) Almost any evening there is a wealth of glamorous musical events for you to choose from: the Czech Philharmonic Orchestra and local chamber-music ensembles, as well as opera programmes at the National Theatre and the Smetana Theatre. Generous support from the government for the arts means tickets are cheap, providing you buy them from the box-office. The musical pace picks up every year between 12 May and 4 June during the Prague Spring International Music Festival, a pageant of local and foreign orchestras and ensembles, with celebrity soloists and conductors. The choice of venues includes historic churches and palaces.

The **theatre** scene is always busy. The repertoire consists of classical and contemporary dramatists from Sophocles to Shakespeare, or Edward Albee to Tennessee Williams. It is easy enough to find performances in Eng-

The many elements of the "Laterna Magica" spectacle come together in surreal, sellout performances.

lish; consult the *Prague Post* for listings. Otherwise, try one of the pantomime theatres or *Laterna Magika*. If any of the techniques of the multi-media Magic Lantern spectacle seem familiar, remember that they were invented here, beginning in the 1950s. The exciting blend of music, mime, ballet, and film, humour, and surrealism is always a sellout. The best performances are advertised at the Nová Scéna, next to the National Theatre.

Folklore and theatre performances are presented daily at 7:30 P.M. in July and August on Slovanský Island (also not far from the National Theatre).

Prague has many good **jazz clubs,** such as the Reduta (Národní 20) and the Agharta (Krakovská 5). Arrive by 8:00 P.M. if you want to get a seat. As for **nightclubs,** avoid those on Wenceslas Square, which have high entrance fees and a tacky atmosphere. Try Malostranská Beseda (Mal-

Prague has plenty of cultural diversions to suit your mood, from classical drama to traditional Bohemian folk dance.

ostranská Square) or Radost (Bělehradská 120). For far more tranquil nightlife you can find many candlelit wine restaurants (*vinárny*) with soft music and good food.

Cinemas abound all around Wenceslas Square. Foreign films are often shown with Czech subtitles. Avoid the movies listed with a small square symbol alongside the title; they have been dubbed into Czech. Seats are reserved, so it's best to book early.

SHOPPING

Items marked *PRODEJ* are on sale.

In some cities—London, Rome, and Hong Kong, for example—shopping is one of the main events. Prague is not in the same league, but things have greatly improved since 1989, and you should enjoy browsing around the capital's department stores and boutiques. Window-shopping is particularly pleasurable along the "King's Road" of Prague, the progression of historic streets leading from the Powder Tower in the Old Town all the way to Prague Castle.

For an overall picture of what's for sale in Prague, take your own unguided tour of one of the big department stores, Kotva or Bílá labut. As well as toothpaste and light bulbs you will find everything from furniture, fabrics, sports equipment, and clothing to tourist souvenirs.

A display of Matryoshka dolls, which are popular Czech souvenirs.

Handicrafts ranging from bric-à-brac and trinkets to fine embroidery and ceramics are sold at state-run shops such as Krásná jizba, Česká jizba, and Dílo (which specializes in art).

For most gift buyers, the Czech Republic means **crystal** and **glassware.** Shops selling the standard range of glass and crystal items abound along the main tourist routes. The best-known brand names are Moser (founded in Karlsbad in the 19th century) and Bohemia.

Porcelain is also an equally promising area. If you're not in the market for a 110-piece, hand-painted dinner service, do consider a porcelain figure. Classic Bohemian porcelain in the characteristic cobalt-blue "onion" design can be found at the Český Porcelán factory outlet in the Old Town.

Charming hand-made **marionettes** are widely available, representing dramatic or melodramatic figures. There are, of course, plenty of **dolls** in regional costumes, carved wooden dolls, and angels.

Embroidery is well represented in the gift shops, especially tablecloths and napkins in colourful folkloric patterns.

Be sure to look out for classic Bohemian **garnets** (*České granáty*)—clusters of semi-precious stones made up into brooches, bracelets, or chains.

For a liquid souvenir, you should consider a **bottle** of *Becherovka*, the aperitif from Karlovy Vary ("since 1807"), or one of the more potent native drinks, such as smooth *slivovice* (plum brandy).

Finally, since Prague is such a musical capital, **compact discs** and **cassette tapes** make interesting (as well as economical) souvenirs. Lend an ear to the locally produced classics, opera, folklore, and pop.

SPORTS

For a small country, the Czech Republic has produced an improbably plenteous crop of international **tennis** stars. Their names, however complex, trip from the tongues of sports fans

Beautiful Bohemian crystal and coloured glassware make attractive souvenirs.

everywhere. The secret, apparently, is a rigorous nation-wide talent hunt and training programme, a modern approach to a very traditional Bohemian sport (the first

Calendar of Events

For the most up-to-date information on the city's festivals and arts calendar, consult the tourist information office and local listings in *Prague News* or the *Prague Post*. Look out too for fly posters advertising local happenings. The following list gives a flavour of some of the major events.

January
Spectacular New Year celebrations all across the city.

April–October
Křižík's fountain, Holešovice, Prague Exhibition Grounds. Spectacular light show performances every evening in the open-air theatre at Křižík's fountain.

12 May–4 June
Prague Spring Festival (*Praské jaro*), various city venues. Major international classical-music festival.

July–August
Prague Verdi Festival, colourful displays of folklore music, dance, and traditional costumes from Bohemia and Moravia.

September
Prague Autumn Festival, Municipal House. An international music festival. Concert season begins in earnest.

October
International Jazz Festival, which takes place in odd years, i.e., every other year.

December
Advent and pre-Christmas festivities, open-air arts and crafts market.

tennis tournament hereabouts was held in 1879). To see future stars practising, take a look at the big modern tennis complex on Štvanice Island, in the Vltava River beneath the Hlávkův Bridge. You may be able to play there, too, but only by reserving a court in advance (tel. 231 63 23). Additional public courts can also be found in the Letná Gardens (tel. 37 36 83).

As for **golf**, there's a nine-hole course at Motol, Prague 5 (tel. 651 2464). More elegant is the 18-hole layout at the historic spa of Mariánské Lázně; tel. 0165 4300. For **mini-golf,** try the Výstaviště exhibition grounds in Holešovice, Prague 7 (tel. 37 73 41).

The country's most popular **spectator sports** are football (soccer), ice hockey, basketball, and volleyball. Possibly the last word in sports stadiums is the Strahov installation in Břevnov, Prague 6. For gymnastic occasions there is room enough on the field for 16,000 sportsmen and women. The adjoining football stadium seats a mere 56,000 spectators.

Horse racing takes place every Sunday from April to the end of October at Velká Chuchle, Prague 5. Every year in October a famous steeplechase is run at Pardubice, about 80 km (50 miles) east of Prague. More than 50,000 spectators come out to watch the race, and perhaps wager a few crowns on the outcome.

CHILDREN'S PRAGUE

The Prague **Zoo** (*Zoologická zahrada*) will appeal to many children, whatever their age. The spacious, forested setting, out of the way in Troja, Prague 7, gives a certain freedom to the more than two thousand animals. The most unusual inhabitants here are the Przewalski horses, handsome, white-muzzled natives of Asia, now extinct in the wild but bred successfully in the zoo.

Boat trips on the Vltava start from the quay just north of Palacký Bridge. All the excitement attracts dozens of inquisitive swans, who graciously accept handouts. The excursion itineraries, subject to river conditions, are usually suspended in winter. Farther north, rowing boats may be hired on Slovanský Island (near the National Theatre).

Older children will enjoy several of Prague's **museums,** such as the National Technical Museum, with its collection of historic bi-

Prague offers many diversions for the younger set.

cycles, cars, trains, and planes. The National Museum shows mineralogical, botanical, and zoological collections, among others, and there's even a giant whale's skeleton on display. Artefacts from the cultures of American Indians and Eskimos are displayed at the Náprstek Museum (*Náprstkovo muzeum*), which also exhibits a rich collection of statuettes and native masks that hail from Africa and Oceania.

Children will also love the Prague Exhibition grounds at Výstaviště in the summertime, which include a funfair, planetarium, theatre, open-air cinema, different exhibitions, and several restaurants, as well as a special musical fountain display.

EATING OUT

Prague offers the perfect antidote to the rigours of health food and *nouvelle cuisine*: honest, filling, often delicious dishes, based on the kind of recipes grandmother kept to herself. Since the "velvet revolution," there has been a significant increase in the range of international cuisine on offer. Nowadays, fresh fruit and vegetables are much more available than a few years ago, so you're never in danger of going away hungry.

The hearty Czech cuisine is typically based around roasted pork or beef with, almost invariably, dumplings to soak up the gravy. Or your appetite may point to poultry, game, or fish. The generally heavy, savoury food goes down best of all with cold Czech beer, a brew admired for centuries by gourmets everywhere.

The atmosphere in Prague's eating places is often colourful or romantic, though the standard of service is variable. The waiters might be efficient or friendly, and sometimes both, but in a number of restaurants the employees might neglect their customers.

Where To Eat

A selection of recommended eating establishments is given on page 136–143. Eating places, with which Prague is generously endowed, are divided into categories and then graded from one plus (luxurious) to four, according to the level of the facilities. For technical reasons, many good

Outdoor dining — Prague offers a wealth of inspiring lunchtime locations and the chance to indulge a hearty appetite.

restaurants get no more than a second-class seal of approval (written as *II. cenová skupina*); but don't let that stop you from sampling their fare.

Apart from conventional restaurants (called *restaurace*), which may be exclusive or geared to a regional or foreign cuisine, the following options are worth seeking out:

Vinárny ("wine restaurants") may have the same menus as ordinary restaurants, but they highlight the wine accompanying the food. The ambience is often intimate, and possibly historic or folkloric as well.

Pivnice or *hospoda* (pubs or taverns) specialize in draught beer and a limited variety of traditional meat platters; the mood is likely to be jolly, with informal service.

Kavárny (cafés) are essentially for snacks and sweet pastries, though you may find some hot meals on the menu.

If you're in a rush and need a quick snack, there is now a wide range of cheap fast-food outlets and self-service bistros in the city centre.

Anti-smoking activists will be pleased with Prague, where smoking in restaurants tends to be banned at lunchtime. This doesn't affect pubs, however.

Breakfast

Breakfast (*snídaně*) is served by hotels from about 6:00 A.M. to 10:00 A.M. Depending on the establishment the meal can be as simple as bread, butter, and jam with coffee and tea, or as beautiful as you could wish. In the better hotels, a lavish hot and cold buffet is served. Another option is to eat out at one of the growing number of American-influenced diners. For tasty, imaginative, and inexpensive

Eating and drinking are taken seriously in Prague, as shown by this detail on a building in Mala Strana.

fare, try the Red, Hot, and Blues (Jakubská 12) in the Old Town, or Cornucopia (Jungmannová 10).

Lunch and Dinner

Most restaurants post a typewritten menu (*jídelní lístek*) near the door, giving you an idea of the prices, at least. At the self-service counter you needn't know the language; just point to what you want. However, nowadays, most cheap and medium-priced as well as first-class restaurants tend to have menus in English and German as well as Czech.

The menu is divided into categories such as these: *studená jídla* (cold dishes), *polévky* (soups), *teplé předkrmy* (warm

starters, or appetizers), *ryby* (fish), *drůbež* (poultry), *hotová jídla* (main courses), and, to finish, *moučníky* (desserts).

The supreme **starter** here is Prague ham (*Pražská šunka*), a succulent local speciality. It may be served in thin slices, garnished with cucumber and horseradish, or with cheese in miniature sandwiches.

Soup is a popular choice at both lunch (*oběd*) and dinner (*večeře*). It may be a fairly light bouillon or, more likely, a thick, wholesome soup of potatoes, vegetables, and perhaps a bit of meat. A dab of whipped cream may also be added. One of the heartiest traditional recipes is *bramborová polévka s houbami* (potato soup with mushrooms). The name hardly does justice to the thick soup flavoured with onion, lard, carrots, cabbage, parsley, and spices.

Meat dishes include succulent *Pražská hovězí pečeně* (Prague roast beef), a joint of beef stuffed with fried diced ham, peas, egg, onion, and spices. Also, look for *svíčková pečeně na smetaně*, tasty beef in a cream sauce. Some hotel restaurants offer an inspired variant on a simple theme, *vepřové žebírko Interhotel* (pork chops à l'Interhotel), the chops stuffed with a mixture of sauerkraut, ham, and bacon.

> **Certain dishes (mostly meat dishes) can be ordered only after 6pm.**

Another gourmet adventure is *šunka po staročesku* (old Bohemian-style boiled ham), involving a sauce of plums, prunes, walnut kernels, and wine. For memories of the Austro-Hungarian Empire, you should sample some *guláš* (goulash), a meat stew flavoured with paprika sauce, or *smažený řízek* ("Wienerschnitzel"), a breaded veal cutlet. Just about any of these dishes may be accompanied by *knedlíky* (dumplings) and *kyselé zelí* (sauerkraut).

Desserts are usually in the heavyweight category, with tasty dishes like *jablkový závin* (apple strudel), with a topping of whipped cream. A slightly more delicate variation, *jablka v županu* (apple baked in flaky pastry), uses whole apples stuffed with sugar, cinnamon, and raisins. *Švestkové knedlíky* (plum dumplings) are sprinkled with curd cheese and sugar, and then doused in melted butter. A great favourite is *palačinka*, ice cream or cream and fruit enveloped in a pancake. Or perhaps settle for *zmrzlina* (ice cream) or *kompot* (stewed fruit).

> Cheers! –
> *Na zdraví*
> (nahsdrahvee)

Vegetarians

The presence of a large expatriate community has ensured the emergence of several vegetarian cafés and restaurants over the past few years. Consequently, many non-vegeta-

Prague's Bierfest draws crowds of devoted locals, and thirsty visitors as well.

rian restaurants also now offer a range of options *bez masa* (without meat).

One of the best places for vegetarian food is the Palace Hotel Cafeteria (Panská 12), open from noon until 9:00 P.M. Although the cafeteria is self-service, the standard of food is consistently high, and it has the best salad bar in town, with the added advantage of being smoke-free.

Snacks

In-between meals in Prague you will no doubt be tempted by the inventive array of inexpensive snacks sold at street stands. A *bramborák* is a savoury potato pancake, served greasily but deliciously on a piece of paper. *Pečená klobása* (roasted sausage) rates a paper plate, a slice of bread, and a squirt of mustard, but no fork or knife. *Smažený sýr* is a sort of vegetarian Wienerschnitzel, consisting of fried cheese. A huge number of American-style fast-food outlets have begun to spring up, particularly along and around Wenceslas Square, where there's a roaring nightly trade in sausages served with a dollop of mustard and hunks of brown bread. Nowadays, ice cream is sold everywhere, most commonly from hole-in-the-wall cone dispensaries.

Drinks

Prague offers a wonderful selection of places to drink — and very many of them will provide light meals as well. The architectural richness of the city ensures a range of superb settings, added to which the thriving café society of the early 20th century is now beginning to re-emerge.

Karlovy Vary, known for the healing power of its mineral water, has attracted an illustrious crowd over the centuries.

When the international statisticians turn their attention to **beer** (*pivo*), the Czech Republic usually comes in among the top two or three countries in the world for per capita consumption. Once you taste the local brew on the spot, you'll understand why. The kind of connoisseurs who go to Burgundy for wine-tasting pilgrimages should plan a journey to Plzeň (Pilsen), in the west of the Czech Republic, for the brewer's equivalent. Pilsner beer, which has been produced since the 13th century, is a species of lager admired and copied far and wide. Experts attribute its distinctive flavour to the alkaline water and the excellence of a key ingredient, hops, which grow on vast wood-and-wire frames in the Bohemian countryside.

Pilsner beer is perhaps the most widely known, but there are many other well-regarded breweries in Prague and the smaller towns. Several Prague pubs brew their own, light (*světle*) or dark (*tmave*). As tasty and refreshing as it may be, do keep in mind that it's probably stronger than the brews you're used to.

Czech **wine** (*vino*) is almost unknown abroad, so you're bound to discover something new without having to look very hard. Bohemia produces only a small proportion of the country's total wine output, most coming from south Moravia. Bohemian wines are reminiscent of German wines. White is *bílé* and red is *červené*.

A drink local to Karlovy Vary, *Becherovka is* made of herbs and served chilled as an aperitif, as is the powerful, sweetish *Stará myslivecká*. After-dinner drinks generally mean fruit brandies, especially *slivovice*, which is made from plums.

Non-alcoholic drinks include pure mineral water, fruit juices, and international brands of soft drinks. Turkish coffee and Italian-style espresso are also very popular.

To Help You Order...

Could we have a table?		**Máte prosím volný stůl?**	
The bill, please.		**Zaplatím.**	
I'd like ...		**Prosím ...**	
beer	**pivo**	meat	**maso**
bread	**chleba**	the menu	**jídelní lístek**
butter	**máslo**	milk	**mléko**
cheese	**sýr**	mineral water	**minerálku**
coffee	**kávu**	salad	**salát**
dessert	**moučník**	sugar	**cukr**
egg	**vejce**	tea	**čaj**
ice cream	**zmrzlinu**	wine	**víno**

...and Read the Menu

bažant	pheasant	**knedlíky**	dumplings
brambory	potatoes	**králík**	rabbit
drůbež	poultry	**kuře**	chicken
fazole	beans	**květák**	cauliflower
houby	mushrooms	**kyselé zelí**	sauerkraut
hovězí	beef	**ledvinky**	kidneys
hrášek	peas	**pstruh**	trout
hrozny	grapes	**rajská jablka**	tomatoes
hrušky	pears	**rýže**	rice
husa	goose	**špenát**	spinach
jablka	apples	**srnčí**	venison
jahody	strawberries	**štika**	pike
játra	liver	**šunka**	ham
jazyk	tongue	**švestky**	plums
jehněčí	lamb	**telecí**	veal
kachna	duck	**telecí brzlík**	sweetbreads
kapr	carp	**vepřové**	pork
klobása	sausage	**zajíc**	hare

INDEX

HANDY TRAVEL TIPS

An A–Z Summary of Practical Information

Prague

Listed after some entries is the appropriate Czech translation, usually in the singular, plus a number of phrases that may come in handy during your stay in the Czech Republic. For a guide to pronunciation, see LANGUAGE.

A

ACCOMMODATION (See also CAMPING, YOUTH HOSTELS, and the selection of RECOMMENDED HOTELS)
Hotels are officially classified according to the scope and standard of their services, from five stars for the most luxurious to one star for the most basic. To earn the five-star *de luxe* rating a hotel must have superior rooms and elaborate facilities of the sort expected by international business people, such as translation and secretarial services, a fitness centre, shops on the premises, and multiple bars and restaurants. In fact, some hotels with fewer stars outdo the more exclusive modern palaces in architectural charm and friendly service. One-star hotels truly have no frills.

Package tours usually include breakfast and dinner or full board; in some cases the commitment may be reduced to breakfast only.

It's advisable, though not essential, to book accommodation well in advance, as the principal hotels are often filled to capacity between April and mid-November and during festivals and congresses. Although many new hotels have been built in Prague in recent years, they are mostly swish and expensive, so if you go on spec, you may pay far more than you had bargained for. If you arrive without a reservation, try Pragotour in Za Poříčskou branou 7 (tel. 231 11 16 or 24 81 61 20, fax 24 81 61 72), which organises car rental as well as hotel and youth-hostel bookings. You could also go to one of the reservation centres of Čedok, the country's biggest travel agency, at Na příkopě 18; tel. 24 19 76 15. However, be warned that Čedok's prices may be significantly higher than those of other agencies, and non-refundable deposits are required.

If you arrive by train, contact the excellent A.V.E. travel agency situated in the main railway station (Hlavní nádraží; tel. 24 22 32 21/6). They can arrange hotel rooms and hostel accommodation as well as private self-catering apartments, and are open from 6am to 11pm. Another office is at Holešovice station. For self-catering apartments and houses, also try the Prague Suites agency in Melantrichová.

Young people can head for the C.K.M. (Youth Travel Bureau) agency at Žitná 12 (tel. 29 12 40, fax 24 21 62 10) between 8am and 6pm for information on available spaces in Prague's hostels and budget hotels. There's a Juniorhotel at the same address providing basic accommodation for anyone under 30.

Botels. For an efficient alternative to a conventional hotel you can stay in a converted river-boat, called a "botel." Prague has three of these floating hotels permanently moored along the Vltava. The amenities rate three stars.

I'd like a single room/ double room.	**Chtěl bych jednolůžkový pokoj/dvoulůžkový pokoj.**
with bath/with shower	**s koupelnou/se sprchou**
What's the rate per day?	**Kolik stojí za den?**

AIRPORT *(letisté)*

Prague-Ruzyně airport, less than 20 km (12 ½ miles) from the city centre, is served by the Czech airline ČA and more than 20 foreign lines. In addition to its international role, Prague is the transit point for flights to Brno and other airports around the country.

Facilities include a bureau de change, cash-point, accommodation, information point, post office, car-rental desk, café, and restaurant. There are also a few souvenir and duty-free shops. Luggage trolleys (baggage carts) are free, and there are porters on hand to help.

Ground transport. Taxis by the dozen are available for arriving passengers, but often charge three times the accepted rate. Buses 119 and 254 run frequently to Dejvická, which connects with the metro.

Prague

A microbus is the recommended transport to city centre. They leave at regular intervals from the Czech Airlines Center.

Departure. For the correct check-in time, consult your airline or the ČA office. If you arrive at the airport early, note that once you have checked in, you will no longer be allowed to stay with friends or family who have come to see you off.

Where do I get the bus to the city centre?/to the airport?	**Odkud jede autobus do centraměsta?/na letiště?**
Porter!	**Nosič!**
Take these bags to the bus/taxi, please.	**Prosím, odneste tato zavazadla k autobusu/taxi.**

C

CAMPING

Several campsites aimed at economy-minded vacationers are found in areas near central Prague, such as Troja and Braník. Don't expect luxury: the standard of facilities is rated no higher than average. To make reservations contact the PIS Information Service at Na příkopě 20. Campsites with bungalows for hire are:

Sportcamp, Nad hliníkem 15, Prague 5; tel. 52 18 02, fax 52 16 32.
Kotva Intercamp, U ledáren 55, Prague 4; tel. 46 60 85, fax 46 61 10.
There is also Caravancamp at Plzeňská, Prague 5; tel. 52 47 14, fax 52 16 32.

CAR HIRE/RENTAL *(pjçovna auto)* (See also DRIVING and MONEY MATTERS)

In Prague, car-rental agencies include Budget, at the Hotel Inter-Continental; tel. 24 88 11 11; Europcar, Pařižská 26; tel. 24 81 05 15; and Avis, at Klimentská 46; tel. 21 85 25/6, fax 21 85 12 29. Other Pragocar offices are located at the airport, the Hilton, International, President, Kampa, Slavia, and Forum Hotels. Čedok (Na příkopě office) also arranges car hire; tel. 24 19 71 11, fax 232 16 56.

You can rent a wide range of economy and luxury cars, both Czech and foreign. You have the choice of a standard tariff per hour or day and an unlimited-mileage rate which includes collision damage waiver. The requirements and paperwork are about the same as in any other country, with the most convenient method of payment by credit card. It is illegal to drive in the Czech Republic with even a drop of alcohol in your bloodstream.

Although all the operators generally speak English, the following phrases might be useful:

I'd like to hire a car.	**Chtěl bych si půjčit auto.**
large/small	**velké/malé**
for one day/a week	**na jeden den/týden**
Please include full insurance.	**Prosím, započítejte plné pojištění.**

CLIMATE and CLOTHING

Prague is a four-seasoned city with a continental climate. The summers tend to be sunny and quite hot, the winters cold, spring and autumn mild but changeable.

The following chart indicates the average monthly temperatures in Prague:

		J	F	M	A	M	J	J	A	S	O	N	D
Maximum	°F	50	52	64	73	82	88	91	90	84	71	57	50
	°C	10	11	18	23	28	31	33	32	29	22	14	10
Minimum	°F	9	10	18	28	36	45	48	46	39	28	23	14
	°C	-13	-12	-8	-2	2	7	9	8	4	-2	-5	-10

In summer lightweight clothing is recommended, though a jacket or sweater might come in handy in the evening. Winters are quite cold, so you will need an overcoat and heavy shoes. Rainwear is useful throughout much of the year.

Prague

Casual attire is fine for most occasions, though business circles tend towards sober suits. In the evening a certain amount of formality is appropriate, especially if you're going to the opera or the theatre, where locals sometimes wear evening dress. Incidentally, public places have vast cloakroom (hat check) facilities, which should be used. It's considered *nekulturní*—literally "uncultured"—to wear or carry a hat or coat into a restaurant or theatre.

COMMUNICATIONS (See also Opening Hours)

Post Offices (*posta*). Post offices deal with mail, faxes, telegrams, telex, and telephone service. Postage stamps are also available where postcards are sold. Post boxes, attached to buildings, are orange facing the street but blue on the sides, with a slot in each of the sides. The historic main post office at Jindřišská 14, Prague 1, is open 24 hours a day. If you want to send a package abroad, you may need to go to the customs office (8 Sokolovska 22) if its contents are subject to export restrictions.

Poste Restante/General Delivery. If you're going to be in Prague long enough to receive mail, but don't know where you'll be staying, you can have letters addressed to you poste restante (the same expression is used in the Czech Republic as in Britain). Have your mail addressed to c/o Poste Restante, Jindřišská 14, Prague 1, Czech Republic. Pick up your mail at the main post office, and don't forget to take along your passport for identification.

Telegrams (*telegram*) and **faxes** may be sent from post offices and from the business centres of modern major hotels. **Telex** services are available at the main post office and at large hotels.

registered/air mail	**doporučeně/letecky**
I'd like a stamp for this letter/postcard, please.	**Prosím známku na tento dopis/lístek.**
I'd like to send a telegram.	**Chci poslat telegram.**

Telephone *(telefon)*. Most telephones in Prague are now operated by phone cards *(telecart)* rather than coins, and the coin-operated ones tend to be out of order. Phone cards are widely available from newsagents, tobacconists, post offices, and streetsellers. The cheapest of these costs 150 Kč. Using a card to telephone abroad is expensive, however — it will probably cost more to call London from Prague than vice versa. To make international direct-dial calls: 00 + country code + city code + number.

For international calls without the coin or card problem, try the telephone centre at the main post office (where you pay a deposit and square up later) or your hotel (where you will be liable to a hefty surcharge). The international operator is reached by dialling 0131, 0132, 0133, or 0135.

Note: Telephone numbers in Prague are gradually being changed; you must check with the operator if you experience problems obtaining a number.

Can you get me this number in …? **Můžete mne spojit s tímto telefonním číslem v …?**

COMPLAINTS

If you have a serious complaint about business practices, first try talking to the manager of the establishment. Should this not resolve the problem, ask the Prague Tourist Centre for advice (see page 123).

CRIME (See also EMERGENCIES and POLICE)

Violent crime is still low by the standards of western Europe or the United States, but there is a great deal of theft. Lock your car and put your valuables in the hotel safe. Be alert to the danger of pickpockets in crowded places, particularly on trams and the Metro.

I want to report a theft. **Chci ohlásit krádež.**

My wallet/handbag/passport/ **Ukradli mi náprsní tašku**
ticket has been stolen. **(peněženku)/kabelku/pas/lístek.**

Prague

CUSTOMS and ENTRY FORMALITIES

Advance planning is necessary for a trip to Prague. You need a passport (it must be valid for at least another five months) and, if you are visiting from Australia, Canada, New Zealand, or South Africa, a Czech visa (though arrangements may change). Visas are not required by visitors from the U.K., U.S.A., or Ireland. Visas are issued at the airport on arrival, or at the main border points. Otherwise, apply to a Czech embassy or consulate before you go. You must provide your passport, a completed application form (available from some travel agencies), two passport photos, and a visa fee (currently about 1,000 Kč). A visa is normally valid for one visit of up to 30 days. Note that if you intend travelling onwards to Slovakia, you must have a separate visa.

You are permitted to bring into the Czech Republic personal effects for use during your visit. Gifts, too, can be imported without paying duty, so long as they are not of excessive quantity and value. Beyond the usual prohibitions, such as drugs and firearms, there are no other restrictions on what you may import.

Currency restrictions. There is no formal restriction on the amount of foreign currency you're allowed to take into or out of the Czech Republic. However, Czech currency may be imported and none exported.

Duty-free. Allowances going into the **Czech Republic** are as follows: for residents of European countries 250 cigarettes and 50 cigars and 250g of tobacco, 2l of wine, and 1l of spirits; for residents of non-European countries 400 cigarettes or 100 cigars or 500g tobacco, 1l wine and spirits. When returning to your own country you may take the following: **Australia:** 250 cigarettes or 250g of tobacco, 1l of wine or spirits; **Canada:** 200 cigarettes and 50 cigars and 400g tobacco, 1.1l of wine or spirits or 8.5l beer; **New Zealand:** 200 cigarettes or 50 cigars or 250g tobacco, 4.5l wine or beer and 1.1l spirits; **Republic of Ireland:** 200 cigarettes or 50 cigars or 250g tobacco, 2l wine or 1l spirits; **South Africa:** 400 cigarettes and 50 cigars and 250g tobacco, 2l wine and 1l spirits; **U.K.:**

200 cigarettes or 50 cigars or 250g tobacco, 2*l* still wine and 1*l* spirits; **U.S.A.:** 200 cigarettes and 100 cigars and "a reasonable amount of tobacco," 1*l* wine or spirits.

| I have nothing to declare. | **Nemám nic k proclení.** |
| It's for my personal use. | **To mám pro osobní potřebu.** |

D

DRIVING

Entering the Czech Republic. To bring your own car into the country you will need:

- a valid national licence and an international driving permit
- car registration papers
- a form obtainable along with the visa
- a Green Card (an extension to your regular car insurance policy, validating it specifically for the Czech Republic)
- a national identity sticker for the car
- a first-aid kit
- a red warning triangle for use in case of breakdown

If you're driving someone else's car, you must have the owner's written permission.

Speed limits. The maximum is 110 km/h (68 mph) on main highways, 90 km/h (56 mph) on other roads, and 60km/h (37 mph) in towns. The limits are rather strictly enforced. The police levy fines on the spot; if you should have to pay, ask for a receipt.

Driving conditions. Drive on the right, pass on the left. Seat belts must be worn at all times. Alcohol is totally forbidden to drivers; if any amount, however small, is found in the bloodstream it constitutes a serious offence.

For the uninitiated driver, Prague is an obstacle course. Pedestrian zones, one-way streets, detours, and construction projects mean that only people with endless time to spare and expert knowledge — for instance, taxi drivers — feel comfortable driving here. It's even worse during the rush hours, from 6 to 8am and from 3 to 5pm.

In view of the congestion, deviations, and parking restrictions, visitors are advised to leave their cars outside the centre of Prague and use the excellent public transport system from there.

Breakdowns The "yellow angels," mobile mechanics of Autoturist Road Service, come to the aid of motorists in distress; dial 154. There are two garages open round the clock in Prague: at Limuzská 12, Prague 10 and Macurova 1640, Prague 4. Look for emergency telephones on the highway, or dial 158 for the police.

Fluid and Distance charts. See page 128.

Fuel and oil (*palivo; olej*). Most service stations are open from 6am to 8 or 9pm, but 24-hour stations operate in several districts of Prague. Fuel comes in four varieties — special (90 octane), super (96 octane), diesel, and (less widely available) unleaded.

Parking. Prague is trying to provide adequate space for all the cars in short- and long-term car parks in or near the central district. There are also some "human parking meters" who collect a fee for on-street parking. If you leave your car in a restricted zone, it will probably be clamped (booted) and you will have to pay a heavy fine.

Road signs. Most road signs are standard international pictographs, but here are some written ones you may come across:

Jednosměrný provoz	One way
Na silnici se pracuje	Road works (Men working)
Nebezpečí	Danger
Nevstupujte	No entry
Objížďka	Diversion (Detour)
Opatrně	Caution
Pěší zóna	Pedestrian zone
Pozor	Attention

Snížit rychlost (zpomalit)	Slow down
Vchod	Entrance
Východ	Exit

Full tank, please.	**Plnou nádrž, prosím.**
super/normal/unleaded/diesel	**super/obyčejný/ bezolovnatý/nafta**
Check the oil/tyres/battery, please.	**Prosím, zkontrolujte mi olej/pneumatiky/baterii.**
I've broken down.	**Mám poruchu.**
There's been an accident.	**Stala se nehoda.**
Can I park here?	**Mohu zde parkovat?**
Are we on the right road for …?	**Jedeme dobře do …? (Vede tato silnice do …?)**

E

ELECTRIC CURRENT

In almost all the places a tourist might stay in Prague the power is 220-volt, 50-cycle AC. American appliances will need transformers and plug adaptors.

EMBASSIES and CONSULATES *(konzulát, vyslanectví, velvyslanectví)*

To find the address and telephone number of any diplomatic representative in Prague, look in the telephone directory under "Zastupitelské úřady." The main ones for English-speaking visitors are:

Canada	Mickiewiczova 6, Prague 6; tel. 24 31 11 08
United Kingdom	Thunovská 14, Prague 1; tel. 57 32 03 55
U.S.A.	Tržiště 15, Prague 1; tel. 57 32 06 63

Office hours are from 8 or 8:30am to 4 or 4:30pm.

EMERGENCIES (See also EMBASSIES and CONSULATES, MEDICAL CARE, and POLICE)

In an emergency you can dial the following numbers 24 hours a day:

Police	**158**
Fire	**150**
Emergency first aid	**155**
Dental emergency service	**24 23 03 88**
Careful!	**Opatrně!/Pozor!**
Fire!	**Hoří!**
Help!	**Pomoc!**
Stop thief!	**Chytte zloděje!**

G

GAY and LESBIAN TRAVELLERS

Prague has a lively gay and lesbian scene which accords everyone a friendly welcome. Places to try are the Club U Petra Voka (Na bělidle 40, Prague 5), the Tropic (Jeruzalémská 13, Prague 1), and the Riviera (Národní 20).

GUIDES and TOURS (See also MONEY MATTERS)

As well as Čedok and Pragotur, a number of private agencies offer a wide range of multi-lingual guided tours of short and long duration, from a three-hour orientation tour of Prague to excursions all around the Czech Republic. Themed tours are available, such as historic and Jewish Prague, and you can choose from a bewildering array of boat trips and cruises. Nightbirds can opt for an evening tour of the city, which includes a visit to a typical pub. The more adventurous can even take to the skies in a hot air balloon for a bird's-eye view of Prague's splendours. Agencies are also able to arrange an individual guide/interpreter. Some of the hotels, as well as Čedok, can provide qualified translators or interpreters for business visitors.

L

LANGUAGE

The national language is Czech. The most widely studied foreign languages are English and German. If Slavic languages are Greek to you, don't worry—English is widely spoken, though an understanding of German may help. If you can learn a few Czech words, it will always be appreciated.

The Czech alphabet has 33 letters; for instance, *c* and *č* are counted as two different letters. Here are a few tips on the pronunciation of the more difficult sounds:

ţ like *ty* in not yet	č like *ch* in **ch**urch
ň like the *n* in Ca**n**ute	ch like English *h*
š like the *sh* in **sh**ine	j like *y* in **y**ellow
ž like the *s* in plea**s**ure	ř like *rs* in Pe**rs**ian
c like *ts* in **ts**etse	

The Berlitz CZECH PHRASE BOOK AND DICTIONARY covers most situations you are likely to encounter during your visit to the Czech Republic.

Do you speak English?	**Mluvíte anglicky?**
I don't speak Czech.	**Nemluvím česky.**
Good morning/Good afternoon	**Dobré jitro/Dobré odpoledne**
Good evening/Good night	**Dobrý večer/Dobrou noc**
Please	**Prosím**
Thank you	**Děkuji Vám**
Thank you very much	**Velice Vám děkuji**
That's all right/You're welcome.	**To je ve pořádku.**

LAUNDRY and DRY CLEANING

The easiest way to deal with the problem is to hand over your laundry to your hotel maid. Less expensively, you can pay a visit to the neighbourhood laundry (*prádelna*) or dry cleaner (*čistírna*). Express laundries can wash, dry, and press your clothes within 24 hours.

Prague

Coin-operated launderettes are not common. Laundry Kings at Dejvická 16 (next to Hradcanska Metro) is open all day every day until 10pm and Laundryland at Londýnská 71, Prague 2 has launderette and dry-cleaning facilities, and will do alterations and repairs.

When will it be ready?	**Kdy to bude hotovo?**
I must have this for tomorrow morning.	**Musím to mít na zítra ráno.**

LOST PROPERTY (See also Police)
In case of any loss, contact the police district department through your hotel (you'll need an interpreter). For lost traveller's cheques, notify the police immediately, then follow the instructions provided with your cheques. If you are stranded with no money, or lose your passport or credit card, contact your embassy (See Embassies and Consulates). Lost credit cards can be reported on the following hotlines: Visa/Diners Club, tel. 24 12 53 53; American Express, tel. 24 21 99 78; Mastercard, tel. 24 42 31 35.

I've lost my passport/wallet/handbag.	**Ztratil jsem pas/náprsní tašku (peněženku)/kabelku.**

MEDIA

Radio and Television. Prague has four radio stations, one of which (Radio Inter) has five-minute news broadcasts in English, French, Spanish, and German every 20 minutes. News in English from the B.B.C. or Voice of America can usually be picked up on short-wave transistor radios.

There are four television channels, all broadcasting in colour. The OK3 channel broadcasts the BBC Breakfast News from 8:30 to 9am during the week as well as programmes from C.N.N. between midnight and 1:30pm. Foreign films are almost always dubbed rather than subtitled. In hotels satellite channels show programmes in their original languages.

Newspapers and periodicals. All main foreign-language newspapers and magazines as well as many tourist publications are available at hotels and news-stands. One of the most informative is the weekly English-language newspaper *Prague Post*, written by English and American staff. It contains news, reviews, comment, and useful addresses, and the classified advertisements are excellent sources of local information. Other publications include the free quarterly *Welcome to Prague*.

Do you have any English-language newspapers?	**Máte nějaké noviny v angličtině?**

MEDICAL CARE (See also EMERGENCIES)
All medical care is provided for a fee to foreign visitors, except for citizens of countries with reciprocal agreements on medical treatment. Treatment facilities will provide receipts for patients to file with their insurance companies.There is a 24-hour emergency medical aid department for foreigners at Na Homolce, Roentgenova 2, Prague 5 (tel. 52 92 21 46). Doctors speak English and German. To call an ambulance, telephone 155—no card or coins are needed from a pay phone. For non-emergency problems, go to the First Medical Clinic of Prague, Vyšehradská 35, Prague 2 (tel. 29 89 78/29 22 86). Emergency dental treatment is available at Palackeho 5, Prague 1. English-speaking visitors can contact the Canadian Medical center (tel. 3165 519) or the American Medical Center (tel. 80 77 56).

Certain pharmacies (*lékárna*) are open after normal business hours; to find the shops on night duty, look for the addresses posted on the door of any pharmacy. If you require certain medicines, it's wise to bring an adequate supply from home, as equivalents may not be available in the Czech Republic. There are pharmacies offering a 24-hour emergency service in every quarter of Prague, including at Štefániková 6, Prague 5, tel. 57 32 09 18. For a list of the rest of the pharmacies contact the Czech Tourist Authority or the Prague Information Centre, tel. 54 44 44.

Where's the nearest pharmacy?	**Kde je nejbližší lékárna?**

Prague

I need a doctor/dentist.	**Potřebuji lékaře/zubaře.**
I have a pain here.	**Bolí mne tady.**
headache/stomach ache	**bolest hlavy/žaludku**
fever/cold	**teplota (horečka)/rýma**

MONEY MATTERS

Currency. The unit of currency in the Czech Republic is the crown (*koruna*), abbreviated Kč. The Czech crown is divided into 100 *hellers* (hal.), though the individual haléř is meaningless.

Coins: 10, 20, 50 hal., 1, 2, 5, 10, 20, 50 Kč.

Notes: 10, 20, 50, 100, 200, 500, 1,000, 2,000, 5,000 Kč.

For currency restrictions, see Customs and Entry Formalities.

Currency-exchange offices (*směnárny*) are everywhere in Prague —at the frontier, the airport, and in town at travel agencies and hotels. Though they may be convenient, they often quote the rate at which they buy rather than sell and add on a hefty commission fee. You will get a much better rate at banks, most of which are to be found in Na příkopě (e.g. Kommerční Banka, Živnostenská Banka). Avoid street money-changers at all costs.

Traveller's cheques may be changed at banks and currency-exchange offices as well as at some souvenir shops, hotels, and restaurants. You'll be asked to show your passport when cashing a cheque. The American Express Travel Service at 56 Wenceslas Square cashes and sells traveller's cheques as well as offering a variety of other services; the office is open from 9am to 6pm Monday to Friday, 9am to noon Saturday. A Thomas Cook bureau on the opposite side of the street has similar facilities.

Credit cards. The use of charge and credit cards is widening, and is almost on a par with countries in the West. The main international credit cards are accepted at travel agency offices, and most hotels and better restaurants as well as some private shops. ATM machines are everywhere as well. Be sure to save all receipts, which you may be required to show on departure.

PLANNING YOUR BUDGET

To give you an idea of what to expect, here's a list of average prices in either Czech crowns (Kč) or U.S. dollars. Remember that all prices must be regarded as *approximate* as inflation continues to rise.

Airport transfer. ČA bus from Prague-Ruzyně airport to Vltava Terminal 20 Kč. Taxi from airport to central Prague 400 Kč.

Buses and metro. Standard fare 8 Kč per trip with no charge, 12 Kč with charge. Passes valid on all lines and vehicles available for 1, 2, 3, 4, 5 days at about 70 Kč/day, one-month pass 380 Kč, three-month pass 1,000 Kč.

Car hire. *economy* 1,500–2,500 Kč per day, 10,000 Kč and up per week. You may also have a small insurance charge.

Cigarettes (packet of 20). Local brands 50 Kč, foreign brands 50–100 Kč.

Entertainment. Opera 400–1200 Kč, concert 300–1500 Kč, nightclub admission 100 Kč.

Hairdressers. *Women*: haircut 200 Kč. *Men*: haircut 100 Kč.

Hotels (double room with bath, including breakfast). *De luxe* 6,000 Kč, standard 4,000 Kč, "cheap" 2,000 Kč.

Meals and drinks. Lunch/dinner in fairly good restaurant 200–300 Kč, coffee 20 Kč, glass of wine 25 Kč, soft drink 20 Kč, beer 25 Kč.

Taxis. In theory, 16 Kč per kilometre is the law; in practice, most tourists are overcharged, so allow extra. Hotel taxis have higher rates.

Tours. City sightseeing (three hours) 300 Kč; river cruise with meal 500 Kč; trips outside Prague to Mělník, various Bohemian castles, or Karlsbad range from 900 to 1,300 Kč, including a meal and a guide.

I'd like to change some pounds/dollars.	**Chci vyměnit nějaké libry/dolary.**
Do you accept traveller's cheques?	**Berete (Přijímáte) cestovní šeky?**
Can I pay with this credit card?	**Mohu platit touto úvěrovou kartou?**

OPENING HOURS

The working day begins early in Prague. **Food shops** start opening up from 6am and may not close until 6pm. **Department stores** and certain other shops do business from 8am to 7pm. Small shops close for a long lunch hour, but the big stores work non-stop. Most stores are open Saturday mornings, and some privately owned enterprises stay open on Sunday.

Banks operate from 8am to noon and 1 to 5pm, Monday to Friday.

Museums are generally open from 9 or 10am to 5 or 6pm daily, except Monday.

PHOTOGRAPHY

Film is relatively expensive, and so is speedy processing. Western brands of film are available from shops displaying the sign "Foto, kino," although these shops are generally closed at the weekend.

Don't take pictures where a sign indicates photography is prohibited (mainly inside historical monuments).

I'd like some film for this camera.	**Prosím film do tohoto aparátu.**
colour print/colour slides	**barevné kopie/barevné diapozitivy**
May I take a picture?	**Smím fotografovat?**

POLICE *(policie)* (See also Emergencies)
The police wear military-style olive-drab uniforms, but you are also likely to see dark green, grey-blue, or black uniforms. White shirts are worn in summer. Police patrol cars are white with the sign "Policie"on either side.

The police emergency telephone number is **158**. The most central police station is at Benediktská 6. If any of your possessions have been stolen, you will need to report the theft to the nearest station for insurance purposes.

Where's the nearest police station? **Kde je nejbližší oddělení Policie?**

PUBLIC HOLIDAYS

1 January	*Nový rok*	New Year's Day
1 May	*Svátek práce*	May Day
8 May	*Vítězství nad fašismem*	Victory over fascism
5 July	*Slovanští věrozvěsti sv. Cyril a Metoděj*	Slavic Missionaries St. Cyril and St. Methodius
6 July	*Výročí úmrtí Jana Husa*	The anniversary of Jan Hus's death
28 October	*První československá republika*	First Czechoslovak Republic
24 December	*Štědrý den*	Christmas Eve
25–26 December	*Svátek vánoční*	Christmas/Boxing Day
Movable date	*Velikonoční pondělí*	Easter Monday

Are you open tomorrow?   **Máte zítra otevřeno?**

R

RELIGION

As you'll soon discover from the proliferation of churches, Prague is a mainly Catholic city. A notice posted at the main entrance gives the times of mass. There are also occasional services in English, French, and German. Look in *Prague Post* for details.

Services in English: Prague Christian Fellowship holds services in English at the Y.M.C.A., Na Poříčí 12, Prague 1, at 6pm on Sunday, except the first Sunday in the month.

Anglican: St. Clement's Church (*Klimentská*), 18 Klimentská, Prague 1, at 11am on Sunday.

Baptist: International Baptist Church of Prague, Vinohradská 68, Prague 3, at 11:30 am on Sunday.

Interdenominational: International Church (*Církev bratrská*), Vrázova 4, Prague 5, at 11:15am on Sunday.

Prague

Jewish: Old-New Synagogue, Maiselova Street, Prague 1, services (in Czech) every weekday 8am, and at 9am on Saturday.

Roman Catholic: Church of St. Joseph, Josefská 4, Lesser Quarter, at 10:30am on Sunday. There are any number of Roman Catholic churches to attend depending on what quarter of Prague you find yourself in. Check with your hotel or in the telephone directory.

T

TIME DIFFERENCES
The Czech Republic follows Central European Time (GMT + 1). From late March until late September clocks are put ahead one hour (GMT + 2). Summer time chart:

Los Angeles	New York	London	**Prague**	Sydney	Auckland
3am	6am	11am	**noon**	8pm	10pm

TIPPING
Tipping is accepted and appreciated. Note that the normal practice in restaurants is to tell the waiter/waitress the full amount you wish to pay when you receive the bill. Do not leave the tip on the table.

Hotel porter, per bag	10 Kč
Hotel maid, per week	50 Kč
Cloakroom (hat check) attendant	2 Kč
Waiter	10%
Taxi driver	10%
Tour guide	50 Kč
Theater usher	5-10 Kč
Keep the change.	**To je dobrý.**

TOILETS/RESTROOMS
Your best bet is to seek out the conveniences in a hotel or restaurant or Metro (underground/subway) station. Toilets are usually sign-posted "WC." Men's facilities will either be marked "Muži" or

"Páni," and women's "Ženy" or "Dámy" or by picture-signs. There may be a standard charge of 1 or 2 Kč in public toilets.

Where are the toilets?   **Kde jsou toalety?**

TOURIST INFORMATION OFFICES

For general and specific information about the Czech Republic, contact the Czech Tourist Authority.

North America: 1109 Madison Avenue, New York, NY 10028; tel. (212) 288-0830, fax (212) 288-0971.

United Kingdom: 95 Great Portland Street, London W1N 5RA; tel. (44171) 291-9920, fax (44171) 436-8300.

In Prague, the main tourist office is at Na příkopě 18, Prague 1; tel. 212 71 11 (open daily 8:30am to 7pm). You can also look for the main office of the **Prague Information Service**, located virtually next door at Na příkopě 20, Prague 1; tel. 54 44 44 (open 9am to 6pm Monday to Friday, 9am to 5pm weekends). The **Prague Tourist Centre**, formerly the American Hospitality Center, will be able to help with general questions and is at the corner of Melantrichova and Rytířská, just beyond Wenceslas Square.

Where's the tourist office?   **Kde je cestovní kancelář?**

TRANSPORT (See also MONEY MATTERS)

Travel passes (*denní jízdenka*) covering periods of one to five days are valid on all forms of public transport in Prague and are an excellent alternative to tickets. They can be purchased from special kiosks marked M.H.D. at major Metro stations (like Můstek, Dejvická, and Hradčanská) and are ideal for exploring the city without having the worry of carrying adequate supplies of small change. For longer-term visitors, a one-month or three-month travel pass (*měsíční jízdenka*) offers substantial savings. You will need photo identification to obtain one. Note that the penalty for travelling without a valid ticket or pass is 200 Kč.

Prague

Metro (underground or subway). Prague's showcase Metro system is clean, bright, fast, and cheap. There are even signboards that tell you how much time has elapsed since the last train departed. Even if you don't need the Metro for getting around, it's worth taking a ride for the experience. The system runs from 5am to midnight.

Metro stations are clearly marked by a stylized "M" symbol pointing downwards. Before you enter, buy a ticket from one of the yellow machines in the entrance hall. This entitles you to an underground ride of any distance, including free transfers among the three Metro lines, within an hour. Remember to validate your ticket by punching it in the machine before entering the platform.

Maps of the Metro system are posted in the stations and inside the trains, while recorded announcements en route identify the stops.

Trams (*tramvay* or *elektrika*). A comprehensive tram (streetcar) network provides cheap surface transport throughout the city and into the outskirts. At each tram stop a chart lists the routes and timetables. Tram tickets are sold at news-stands or from coin-operated machines at stations. When you board, validate your ticket in the machine near the door. Free transfers are not given; you must use a new ticket for each leg of your trip. Some trams run all night at 40-minute intervals. Night tram numbers are white on dark blue.

Buses (*autobus*). Since tram lines efficiently cover the metropolitan area, buses are generally assigned to longer distances. The itineraries are posted at bus stops. There are some night bus routes. On local lines a bus rider needs the same ticket as Metro or tram passengers (see above); validate it in the machine when you board.

Inter-city bus routes link all the main towns. For information on long-distance schedules, telephone 22 14 45/9 (lines are often busy). Tickets for buses to other European cities can be obtained from Čedok, 1. Na příkopě 18, Prague 1, tel. 24 19 71 11, or from Bohemia Travel Service, Vystavište LDS 1/6; tel. 2010 3625.

Taxis. If you have to use a taxi, call the AAA (they speak English), tel. 10 80, or Taxi Praha, tel. 24 91 66 66 0r 24 91 15 59. The taxis on Wenceslas Square tend to be overpriced and your hotel may not call a reputable firm. The meter indicates the fare, but there may be extra charges, for instance for baggage, for night-time journeys, or for leaving the city limits. Before engaging a taxi, ask the rate and make sure the meter works.

Trains. An extensive rail network with first- and second-class service covers the entire country. Trains are generally comfortable but are not always punctual or very clean. Since they tend to get very crowded, it's advisable to book in advance. However, tickets are extremely cheap by Western standards.

Prague has a number of stations, the most frequently used being Hlavní Nádraží and Nádraží Holešovice. For information on train connections, call 24 22 42 00.

I'd like a ticket to …	**Prosím jízdenku do …**
single (one-way)/return	**jednoduchou/zpáteční**
Will you tell me where to get off?	**Prosím, povíte mi kde mám vystoupit?**

TRAVELLERS WITH DISABILITIES

While facilities for the disabled in the Czech Republic are not always up to the standards of other European countries, Prague has nevertheless made some effort to to accommodate the needs of travellers with certain disabilities. A useful contact address is the headquarters of the official national organization for the disabled at Karlínské náměstí 12, Prague 8; tel. 24 21 59 15 (open between 8am and 4pm); staff can supply information as well as hire out wheelchairs for a small daily charge.

Hearing-impaired travellers: contact Audiocentre TV, Františka Křížka 14; tel. 37 78 39, fax 87 85 38. The centre provides a hearing-aid hire service and offers consultation with ear specialists. In the city, light signals at crossroads are designed to help travellers with hearing difficulties negotiate busy junctions. Some theatres, including the National, the Estates, and the Smetana, provide audio-frequency induction loop systems for hearing-aid users.

Sight-impaired travellers: sound signals at major junctions warn sight-impaired travellers of potential dangers. For information on other facilities, contact the official national organization for the disabled at Karlínské náměstí (address above).

A number of hotels have facilities for the disabled, though these tend to be the more expensive ones, such as the Diplomat or the Hilton. It is advisable to make enquiries in advance. Public disabled toilets are in short supply.

TRAVELLING TO PRAGUE
As fares and routes are constantly changing, it's best to consult a dependable, well-informed travel agent for up-to-date information. The following outline suggests some of the varied possibilities.

By air (See also AIRPORT)

Scheduled flights. Prague-Ruzyně airport is well served on international and intercontinental routes by both the Czech airline ČA and foreign companies. Average flying times: New York–Prague 10½ hours; London–Prague 2 hours.

Package tours. The all-in package tour—flight, hotel, and board included—proves a popular way of visiting Prague. Take your choice from a wide variety of packages, from short breaks to a grand tour of the Czech Republic, with Prague as a point of departure. Most tour agents recommend cancellation insurance, a modestly priced safeguard if illness or accident forces you to cancel your holiday.

North American packages featuring a visit to Prague include air fare, transfers, accommodation, sightseeing, and some or all meals. Many tours are organized around a theme (Czech composers) or event (the Prague Spring Festival, for example).

By car (See also DRIVING)
The most convenient route to Prague is the E-50 (Frankfurt-Nuremberg-Pilsen), which crosses the German-Czech border at Waidhaus-Rozvadov (open round the clock). You can also follow the E-55 via Berlin, Dresden, and Chemnitz, entering the Czech Republic at Zinnwald-Cínovec (open 24 hours). Travellers from the British Isles or Ireland have a long haul across the Channel (opt for the Dover-Ostend ferry) and on through Belgium and Germany. The distance from London to Prague is 1,200 km (744 miles). Alternatively, now that the Channel Tunnel is open, travellers from Britain also have the option of taking their cars via the Shuttle service, from London to Paris in under 4 hours.

By coach
This is the cheapest way of getting to Prague. It has a reputation for discomfort, but the journey time of about 20 hours from London is shorter than by train, and most coaches have modern conveniences. Regular services run between Prague and many European cities.

By rail
Travellers from London are advised to take the Eurostar to Paris or Brussels. From Paris, there is a connection to Prague via Stuttgart or Nuremberg; from Brussels you can change at Cologne and travel along the Rhine. There is a fast service to Prague from Berlin which only takes 4 hours. Departures are frequent from Frankfurt, Munich, and Vienna, less so from Rotterdam.

Note that certain Western European rail passes like the Inter Rail card, the Freedom Pass, and Rail Europ S card are now valid for travel in the Czech Republic.

WATER
It is perfectly safe to drink water from the tap anywhere in Prague. Alternatively, try some Czech mineral water, which is bottled at one of the country's well-known spas.

Prague

I'd like a bottle of mineral water. **Prosím láhev minerálky.**
fizzy (carbonated)/still   **sodovku minerálku/přírodn
    minerálku**

WEIGHTS AND MEASURES
The Czech Republic uses the metric system.

Length

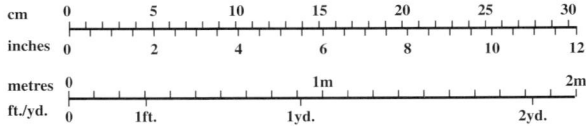

Weight

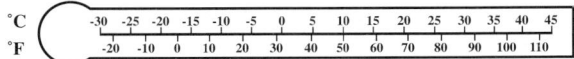

Temperature

Y

YOUTH HOSTELS (See also ACCOMMODATION)
Students should try one of the following organizations:

Student Hostel Strahov, Vaníčkova 5, Prague 6; tel. 52 73 44, fax
52 73 43.

Prague Accommodation Service, Haštalské nám 8, Prague 1, tel.
231 02 02, fax 231 29 43.

Recommended Hotels

Since 1989, Prague has experienced a huge increase in foreign visitors; finding somewhere to stay isn't always easy at certain times of the year. In particular, the number of moderately-priced hotels is in short supply. To help you find your way, we have selected a representative cross-section of the establishments that local sources recommend. We've taken into account the differing requirements of budget holidaymakers and businesspeople, of conservative or adventurous travellers. Our list also includes "botels," attractive hotel barges moored on the Vltava which allow visitors an opportunity to spend the night afloat. For travellers who wish to venture farther afield, we have listed a range of hotels in the delightful spa town of Karlovy Vary.

It's advisable to make advance reservations at Prague hotels. Breakfast and a service charge is normally excluded from the price of the room, and some establishments charge more during special events. As a basic guide to room prices, we have used the following symbols (for a double room per night, with bath or shower, including breakfast) to indicate different categories of establishment, from first class luxury to basic:

✪	3,500 Kč and below
✪✪	3,500–5,500 Kč
✪✪✪	5,500 Kč and above

Club Hotel Praha ✪✪✪ *Průhonice 400, Prague west; Tel. and fax 67 75 08 68*. Located on the main Prague-Brno road, 15 km (9 miles) from the city centre. Delightfully converted building set in attractive parkland. The hotel offers an excellent range of facilities, including two rooms equipped for disabled visitors, a sports centre with squash courts, swimming, 10 tennis courts (specialist coaching is available) and bowling, and a sauna.

Hotel Adria ✪✪✪ *Václavské náměstí 26, Prague 1; Tel. 21 08 11 11; fax 21 08 13 00*. 66 rooms. This newly rebuilt hotel is right in the heart of busy Wenceslas Square.

129

Prague

Hotel Alta Praha ✪✪ *Ortenova náměstí 22, Prague 7; Tel. 80 02 52–9; fax 66 71 20 11.* Though not very central, this hotel is at the cheaper end of Prague's medium-priced range and has good facilities.

Hotel Ambassador-Zlatá Husa ✪✪✪ *Václavské náměstí 5-7, Prague 1; Tel. 24 21 21 85; fax 24 22 61 67.* 180 rooms. Luxurious hotel overlooking Wenceslas Square. Large entertainment complex on site.

Hotel Atlantic ✪✪ *Na poříčí 9, Prague 1; Tel. 24 81 10 84; fax 24 81 23 78.* 61 rooms. Situated in a convenient location close to shops and city sights. Facilities include a restaurant, bar, functions room, and a charming wintergarden.

Hotel Belvedere ✪✪ *Milady Horákové 19, Prague 7; Tel. 20 10 61 11; fax 37 03 55.* 116 rooms and suites. This hotel offers restaurants, bars, a swimming pool, a banqueting hall, and parking facilities.

Hotel Central ✪ *Rybná 8, Prague 1; Tel. 24 81 10 13; fax 232 84 04.* As its name suggests, this hotel is conveniently situated close to the centre of town; at about 2,500 Kč, it is also one of the cheapest.

Hotel Diplomat ✪✪✪ *Evropská 15, Prague 6 ; Tel. 24 39 41 72; fax 24 39 42 15.* 382 rooms and suites. Situated about 3 km (2 miles) outside the centre of Prague, but easily accessible by Metro. The hotel caters for business travellers, but tourists are equally welcome. With all the modern comforts, there is also disabled access as well as 5 rooms adapted for any disabled visitors. Other services include gourmet restaurants, bars and nightclub, business centre, conference facilities, car and limousine hire, fitness centre with exercise room and sauna, and underground parking.

Hotel Esplanade ✪✪✪ *Washingtonova 19; Prague 1; Tel. 24 21 17 15; fax 24 22 93 06.* 64 rooms. Relatively small, stately hotel built in the 1920s. Secluded central location in a quiet street not far from the National Museum and close enough to Wenceslas Square to allow easy access to the city's gems. It is regarded as one of Prague's best hotels, with a highly regarded restaurant.

Hotel Evropa OO *Václavské náměstí 25; Prague 1; Tel. 24 22 81 17; fax 24 22 45 44.* 89 rooms and suites. A very-well-preserved architectural landmark with splendid interior decor from 1889, facing Wenceslas Square. Built by Bělský, the hotel retains its original wood panelling, light fittings, glass, and tiles. Plenty of charm and atmosphere.

Hotel Forum Praha OOO *Kongresová 1, Prague 4 ; Tel. 61 19 11 11; fax 61 21 16 73.* 531 rooms and suites. Glass-and-concrete skyscraper hotel across the road from Palace of Culture. All conveniences, ranging from satellite TV to business centre, limousine service, beer cellar, bowling alley, fitness rooms, and hairdressing salon. Conference facilities are also available on request.

Motel Golf O *Plzeňská 215a, Prague 5 ; Tel. 52 32 51; fax 52 21 53.* No fuss, no frills in this basic motel, though there is a bar and restaurant as well as a golf course.

Hotel Hilton OOO *Pobřežní 1, Prague 8; Tel. 24 84 11 11; fax 24 81 19 32.* 786 rooms and suites with modern facilities. One of the biggest hotels in Prague, this controversial glass construction was built in 1991 and is situated about ½km (1 mile) from the city centre. Facilities include bars and restaurants, a nightclub, extensive conference suites, a casino, fitness centre, and swimming pool.

Hotel Hybernia O *Hybernská 24, Prague 1; Tel. 24 21 04 39.* A small hotel in a very convenient central location near Masarykovo railway station.

Hotel Inter-Continental OOO *náměstí Curieovych, Prague 1; Tel. 24 88 11 11; Fax 24 81 00 71.* 394 rooms and suites. A luxury hotel in the heart of the historic district of Josefov, overlooking the Vltava River, only a short distance from the Old Town Square.

Prague

Modern accommodation in addition to an excellent restaurant, shops, sauna, fitness suite, business services, an underground garage and a nightclub with truly spectacular views of Prague Castle.

Hotel International ✪✪ *Koulova 15, Prague 6 ; Tel. 311 83 00; fax 311 60 31*. Once the meeting place of visiting Soviet communist dignitaries, this 1950s marble-and-granite hotel now specializes in lively beer parties with traditional folk music and loud brass bands. An unusual yet very comfortable hotel, about 3½ km (2 miles) from the centre. Restaurant serves Czech cuisine.

Hotel Jalta ✪✪✪ *Václavské náměstí 45, Prague 1; Tel. 24 22 91 33; fax 24 21 38 66*. 84 rooms and suites. A small luxury hotel facing Wenceslas Square. Excellent accommodation and restaurants serving international cuisine and Moravian wines. There are also bars, nightclubs and a terrace bar for fairweather drinks on the square. The hotel has a renowned casino which plays in Austrian schillings; the exchange office is open all night.

Hotel Juliš ✪✪ *Václavské náměstí 22, Prague 1; Tel. 24 21 70 92*. Situated in the heart of bustling Wenceslas Square.

Hotel Meteor ✪✪ *Hybernská 6, Prague 1 ; Tel. 24 22 06 64*. In a central location near Republic Square, this hotel offers standard accommodation and a restaurant.

Hotel Obora ✪✪ *Libočká 1; Horní Liboc; Prague 6; Tel. 36 77 79;* A charming hotel set in a neat garden beside the wooded grounds of the Star Château, a former royal hunting lodge on the outskirts of Prague. The hotel is managed by a French group.

Hotel Opera ✪ *Těšnov 13, Prague 1; Tel. 231 56 09*. 46 rooms. A truly delightful 19th-century mansion is the setting for this moderately sized hotel, which is located at the edge of a busy road. Good breakfast. Restaurant.

Hotel Paříž ✪✪ *U Obecního domu 1, Prague 1 ; Tel. 24 22 21 51; fax 24 22 54 75.* 96 rooms and 2 luxury suites. A renovated Art Nouveau gem, built originally in 1907, the hotel was declared a national monument in 1984. Its distinctive gargoyles, gables, spires, and turrets give the building a flamboyant air. This is a very popular hotel situated near the Powder Tower; it has a large, enterprising restaurant.

Hotel Praga ✪✪ *Plzeňska 29, Prague 5 ; Tel. 24 51 17 42.* 47 rooms. This pleasant hotel is situated within easy reach of the Mozart museum at Villa Bertramka, and has a bar and restaurant which serves fine Czech and international cuisine.

Hotel Praha (Hyatt) ✪✪✪ *Sušická 20, Prague 6 ; Tel. 24 34 36 50; fax 24 31 04 56.* 124 rooms, 4 apartments and suites. This former retreat for the communist élite was subsumed under American management in 1990. The luxurious hotel is situated approximately 15 minutes' drive from the centre in beautiful gardens with splendid views of the city. There is an excellent restaurant and the Old Prague Beer Club as well as a sauna, swimming pool, and sports facilities.

Hotel President ✪✪ *náměstí Curieových 100, Prague 1; Tel. 231 48 12; fax 231 82 47.* 90 rooms and suites. With its central riverside location, it offers truly spectacular views of Prague Castle. Restaurants, bars, nightclubs, terrace, and casino.

Hotel Splendid ✪ *Ovenecká 33, Prague 7; Tel. 37 33 51; fax 38 23 12.* 35 rooms. This small, comfortable hotel, situated in a delightful street on the left bank near the Prague Exhibition grounds, offers few frills but is excellent value.

Interhotel Panorama ✪✪✪ *Milevská 7, Prague 4 ; Tel. 61 16 11 11; fax 42 62 63.* 451 rooms and suites. Vast modern hotel, distant from the central district but easily reached on the Prague Metro. Luxury facilities include fine French and Czech

Prague

restaurants, bars, sauna, solarium, nightclub, swimming pool, and covered parking.

Juniorhotel ✪ *Žitná 12, Prague 2 ; Tel. 29 29 84; fax 24 22 39 11.* Budget accommodation and basic facilities open to anyone under the age of 30. Often packed out with students or young travellers.

Karl Inn ✪ *Šaldova 54, Prague 8 ; Tel.24 81 17 18; fax 24 81 26 81.* 156 rooms and suites. In a very convenient situation near the Metro, outside the city centre. Facilities include an underground car park and restaurant.

Palace Hotel ✪✪✪ *Panská 12, Prague 1 ; Tel. 24 09 31 11; fax 24 22 12 40.* 125 rooms and suites. One of the most exclusive hotels in the centre of Prague, it is situated just behind Wenceslas Square. The hotel, refurbished in 1991, is still a very prestigious establishment. It was formerly patronized by the European aristocracy, and, special pink rooms with extra mirrors were made for lone female travellers. Superb dining, excellent salad bar, pianobar, casino, and underground parking.

Parkhotel ✪✪ *Veletržní 20, Prague 7; Tel. 20 13 11 11; fax 24 31 10.* 383 rooms and suites. A modern (1960s) hotel situated on the left bank away from central Prague but accessible by Metro. Professional staff and very popular with visitors. Parking.

Pod Lipkami ✪✪ *Pod lipkami 8, Prague 5; Tel. 52 20 28.* 11 rooms. A small, quiet hotel in a secluded suburban area; not too far from the centre of the city. All rooms are equipped with a telephone, bath, and television.

Ungelt Garni ✪✪✪ *Šupartská 1, Staré město, Prague 1; Tel. 24 81 13 30; fax 231 95 05.* 16 suites. This is the only hotel to be found in the central part of the Old Town. Set in a very interesting and historical location, it occupies a wing of the Týn Court, an old medieval warehouse. Breakfast is usually served in the courtyard.

U Raka ✪✪✪ *Černinská 10, Hradčany, Prague 1; Tel. 20 51 11 00; fax 20 51 05 11.* 5 rooms. A charmingly renovated and intimate hotel, conveniently located, and within easy walking distance of Hradčany Square.

BOTELS

Botel Admirál ✪ *Hořejší nábřeží, Prague 5; Tel. 24 51 16 97.* A good range of facilities are available, including a restaurant, and bar, terrace, exchange office and gift shop.

Botel Albatros ✪ *Nábřeží Ludvíka Svobody, Prague 1; Tel. 24 81 05 47.* Conveniently moored close to the city centre, with its own bar and restaurant, summer terrace, exchange office, and gift shop.

Botel Racek ✪ *Na Dvorecké louce, Prague 4; Tel. 61 21 42 42.* Bar, restaurant, terrace, currency exchange office, souvenir shop.

KARLOVY VARY

Bristol Lázeňské Sanatorium ✪✪ *Sadová 19, Karlovy Vary; Tel. (017) 21 31 11, 21 35 14; fax (017) 266 83.* Luxurious accommodation. Facilities include spa and rehabilitation services, medical and dental treatments, sauna, fitness centre, swimming pool, hairdressing salon, and an excellent restaurant (special diets are catered for).

Grandhotel Pupp ✪✪✪ *Mírové náměstí 2, Karlovy Vary; Tel. (017) 221 21, 20 91 11; fax (017) 240 32.* 270 rooms. Large, luxurious hotel in a beautiful setting offering stylish accommodation and excellent facilities. The hotel, a sprawling Baroque and neo-Baroque mansion, was originally established in 1701, was once patronized by the crowned heads of Europe.

Hotel Dvořák ✪✪✪ *Nová louka 11, Karlovy Vary; Tel. (017) 241 45; fax (017) 228 14.* 87 rooms. Very high standard of accommodation set in a historic building, and managed by an Austrian team. Excellent restaurant, sauna, spa centre, and fitness suite.

Recommended Restaurants

Prague has many excellent restaurants to choose from, so to give you some guidance we have made a selection covering a range of locations, types of cuisine and prices. However, restaurants are continually changing, so take local advice or look in the local press for reviews, as no list can be completely up to date.

As a basic guide, we have used the following symbols to give an idea of the price for a three-course meal, for one, including service charge, but excluding wine (drinks, of course, can add considerably to the final bill). It's advisable, as well, to telephone ahead for a table at any of the better restaurants. Unless otherwise specified, the listed restaurants and taverns are open daily. Most now accept major credit cards.

✪	100–200 Kč
✪✪	200–400 Kč
✪✪✪	400–600 Kč
✪✪✪✪	600 Kč and up

FINE DINING

Lobkovická Vinárna ✪✪✪-✪✪✪✪ *Vlašská 17, Prague 1; Tel. 53 01 85.* Open luchtimes and evenings 6:30pm to midnight. On the other side of the river, above Malá Strana, but still very central.

Nebozízek ✪✪✪-✪✪✪✪ *Petřínské sady 411; Tel. 53 79 02.* Open 11am to 6pm and 7pm to 11pm. Closed Monday in winter. Beautifully located halfway up Petřín Hill. The principal attraction is the astounding view of the Old Town and Castle. Cosy and elegant, with menus in Czech and English. There's a summer terrace and garden, too. Reservations are recommended for tables indoors. The best way to get there is by the funicular that runs up Petřín.

Parnas ✪✪✪✪ *Smetanovo nábřeží 2; Tel. 24 22 76 14.* Open noon to 3pm and 4 to 11pm. Candlelit restaurant on the edge of the river, in a convenient situation not far from the Neo-Renaissance building, the National Theatre.

Premiéra ✪✪✪-✪✪✪✪ *U Jinchářích 6; Prague 1; Tel. 24 91 56 72*. Open daily 6-11pm. Excellent fish dishes and, unlike many Czech restaurants, has lamb on the menu.

U Malířů ✪✪✪✪ *Maltézské náměstí 11; Tel. 57 32 03 17*. Open 11am to 3pm and 7 to 10pm. Very expensive restaurant serving French *haute cuisine*. The food and the setting are both wonderful. Perfect for a special occasion.

U Šuterů ✪✪✪✪ *Palackého 4, Prague 1; Tel. 26 10 17*. Open Mon. to Fri. at lunchtimes and daily in the evening until 11:30pm. Sea-bass, sweetbreads with truffles, Belgian beer, and the chance to cook your own meat, should you so wish.

Vinárna U Sixtů ✪✪✪ *Celetná 2; Tel. 24 22 57 24*. Open noon to 1am, this restaurant is conveniently situated near the Old Town Square. Specialities include delectable Moravian and French wines.

Vinárna V Zátisí ✪✪✪ *Liliová 1; Betlémské náměstí; Tel. 24 22 89 77*. Open noon to 3pm and 6pm to 11pm. A highly commendable range of international dishes.

VEGETARIAN

Country Life ✪ *Jungmannová 1; Tel. 24 19 17 39*. Open 9:30am to 6:30pm Monday to Thursday, 10am to 3pm, Friday. This self-service restaurant offers strictly vegetarian and vegan dishes. Also at Melantrichova 15 (tel. 22 53 78; open until 7pm Monday; Sunday noon to 6pm).

FX Café ✪ *Bělehradská 120; Tel. 25 12 10*. Open 11:30am to 5am. An arty café serving designer vegetarian food, including homemade soups, succulent salads, and various tempting desserts. Extremely popular with foreign visitors.

Prague

Palace Hotel Cafeteria ✪ *Panská 12; Tel. 235 75 56.* Open noon to 9pm. The best salad bar in town, so the critics claim. Non-smoking, self-service establishment especially recommended for vegetarians.

TRADITIONAL CUISINE

Myslivna ✪✪✪ *Jagellonská 21, Prague 3; Tel. 62 70 209.* Open daily noon to 4pm and 5pm to midnight. Game specialities such as venison and quail.

Na Rybárně ✪✪-✪✪✪ *Gorazdova 17; Tel. 29 97 95.* Open 4pm to 1am Monday to Friday. An atmospheric little fish restaurant near the Rašínovo embankment, occasionally patronized by President Havel, who lives in a flat nearby. You select the fish yourself before it is cooked, but before you choose the biggest, it's worth knowing that the prices on the menu are per 100g.

U Čížků ✪✪-✪✪✪ *Karlovo náměstí 34; Prague 2; Tel. 29 88 91.* Open noon to 3:30pm and 5pm to 10pm. Attentive service and interesting menu make this charmingly ethnic restaurant popular with foreign visitors in search of authentic cuisine. Reservations advisable.

U Hastrmana ✪✪ *Tel. 29 93 44.* Open daily, 3pm to 1am. Good seafood.

U Mecenáše ✪✪-✪✪✪ *Malostranské náměstí 10; Tel. 53 38 81.* Open 5pm to 11:30pm. Medieval atmosphere — authentic furniture, banners and pictures — in a small Lesser Quarter restaurant noted for good food at honest prices. Reservations essential.

U Pastýřky ✪✪-✪✪✪ *Bělehradská 15, Prague 4; Tel. 43 40 93.* Open every evening until 1am. Log cabin, large beer garden, open hearth on which good steaks and chicken are cooked.

U Pavouka ✪✪ *Celetná 17; Tel. 231 87 14.* Five different sorts of steak and sumptuous Moravian wines in an intimate Gothic underground cellar-restaurant. Bistro upstairs.

U svatého Tomáše ✪✪ *Ietenská 12; Tel. 53 67 76.* Open 11:30am to midnight. A former monastery located in the Lesser Quarter, this restaurant serves dark beer and traditional, if unremarkable, Czech food.

U Mikuláše Dačického ✪-✪✪ *Victoria Huga 2, Prague 5; Tel. 54 93 12.* Mon. to Fri. 4pm to 1am, Sat. 6pm to 1am. Mock-medieval hall painted by Barrandov artists in the 1920s. Interesting venue, though not very central.

U Zelené Žáby ✪✪ *U radnice 8, Prague 1; Tel. 26 28 15.* Open 3pm to 11pm, Sunday to Thursday. Just around the corner from the Old Town Hall, the 15th-century "Green Frog" specializes in excellent Bohemian wines. The house dates from the 12th century.

Valdštejnská Káhospoda ✪✪✪-✪✪✪✪ *Tomášská 16 ; Tel. 53 61 95.* Open 11am to 4pm and 6pm to 11:30pm. Very elegant and refined setting. The *Prague Post* insists that it is recommended by the British ambassador. Some specialities include wild boar, home-made game pâté and rabbit.

Velkopřevorský mlýn ✪✪ *Hroznová 3, Prague 1 (Kampa Island); Tel. 53 30 300.* Open 11am to 11pm. Here, you can enjoy a peaceful atmosphere by the river in the heart of the Lesser Quarter.

Vltava ✪✪ *Nr Palackého most (Palacky Bridge); Tel. 29 49 64.* Traditional Czech fish dishes. Inexpensive and open at lunchtimes as well as in the evening.

TAVERNS AND PUBS

Molly Malones ✪-✪✪ *U obecního dvora 4; Prague 1; Tel. 23 16 222.* Open daily until 1am. Cosy Irish pub in the heart of the Old Town. Good meals.

Slovanský dům ✪ *Na příkopě 22.* Large open courtyard with trees and good beer. Upstairs is the reggae-based nightclub Subway.

U Dvou Koček ✪ *Uhelny tř 10; Tel. 26 77 29, 26 78 18.* In a quiet square near Bethlehem Chapel, the "Two Cats" is a crowded pub with tasty food, good beer, and cheerful service.

U Fleků ✪ *Křemencova 11; Tel. 24 91 51 19.* Open 9am to 11pm. Big, rather tacky but crowded, historic pub features strong dark beer, brewed on the premises. Hearty local food, huge garden and traditional music. An entrance fee is payable.

U Vejvodů ✪ *Jilská 4, Prague 1.* Open daily until 11pm. Very Czech atmosphere with baronial hall interior. In the heart of the Old Town.

INTERNATIONAL

Adonis ✪ *Jungmannová 21.* Good and cheap self-service, in the centre of town. Open during working hours.

Berjozka ✪✪✪ *Rytírská 31; Tel. 22 38 22.* Open 11am to 11pm. The best restaurant in Prague for those who enjoy good Russian food.

Buffalo Bill's ✪✪ *Vodučkova 9; Tel. 24 21 54 79.* Open 11am to 11pm. Relaxed American Southwest decor, Tex-Mex cuisine and country music. Choose among tacos, nachos, quesadillas or burritos and then wash it all down with a marguerita or two. A range of vegetarian entrées is also available.

Dolly Bell ✪✪ *Neklanova 20, Prague 2; Tel. 29 88 15.* Traditional Yugoslav dishes. Particularly recommended is the veal ragout. The upside-down tables hanging from the ceiling add to the excellent atmosphere in this restaurant. Open 2pm to midnight.

Faros ✪✪ *Šporkova 5, Prague 1; Tel. 53 34 82.* A delightful little Greek restaurant in a secluded corner of the Lesser Quarter. Good selection of dishes.

Fakhreldine ✪✪-✪✪✪ *Klimentská 48, Prague 1; Tel. 232 16 59.* Open daily, noon to 11:30pm. Real Lebanese cuisine that cannot fail to please.

La Cambusa ✪✪✪-✪✪✪✪ *Klicterova 2, Prague 5; Tel. 541 16 78.* Northern Italian seafood, flown in daily. Scallops, sea-eel, sea-wolf, octopus. Open Tuesday to Saturday from 7pm. Closed Sunday and Monday.

La Provence ✪✪ *Štupartská 9, Prague 1; Tel. 232 48 01.* Open noon to 11pm. Good French restaurant with reasonable prices.

Pizzeria Kmotra ✪ *V jirchářích 12; Tel. 24 91 5309.* Open 11am to 1am. Café-cum-pizzeria serving beer and enormous pizzas at unbeatable prices. The three-cheese pizza served here is particularly delicious.

Pizzeria Mamma Mia ✪ *Na Poříčí 13, Prague 1; Tel. 232 87 30.* Open until 11pm. Filling pizzas at moderate prices.

Praha Tamura ✪✪✪✪ *Havelská 6, Prague 1; Tel. 24 23 20 56.* Open daily 11am to midnight. Superb fresh Japanese cooking.

Queenz Grill ✪ *Havelská 12, Prague 1.* Inexpensive Middle Eastern finger-food, plus various salads. Open daily until 9pm. Good for a snack while sightseeing.

Reykjavik ✪✪ *Karlova 20; Tel. 26 57 76.* Imaginative menu based on sea fish. Reservations not accepted.

Salammbo ✪✪ *Vyšehradská 21, Prague 2 ; Tel. 29 46 00.* Open daily 11am to midnight. Tunisian cooking.

Shanghai ✪✪ *Moskevská 64, Prague 10; Tel. 72 24 89.* Well-cooked Chinese food at reasonable prices. Open daily until 11pm.

Taj Mahal ✪✪-✪✪✪ *Škrétova 10, Prague 2; Tel. 24 22 55 66.* Open lunchtimes and evenings until 11:30pm. Specialities of Northern and Southern India.

U Golema ✪✪ *Maiselova 8; Tel. 232 81 65.* Open 11am to 10pm, closed weekends. Cosy and intimate restaurant in the Jewish Quarter, offering a range of kosher dishes.

Prague

Viola Trattoria ○○-○○○ *Národní 7; Tel. 24 22 95 93.* Open noon to midnight. Italian restaurant in the heart of the Old Town, not far from the National Theatre. It also offers a nightly programme of poetry readings and jazz. Reservations essential.

CAFÉS

Café Bunkr ○ *Lodecká 2.* Open until 3am. Chic café serving good coffee and live music.

Café u Malostranské věže ○ *Mostecká 3.* Open 10am to midnight. Situated just off Charles Bridge in the Lesser Quarter, this café with Gothic vaults provides refreshing coffee and a good range of wines.

Café Savoy ○ *Vítězná 1.* Open noon to midnight. Exquisite surroundings, soothing music, and attentive waiters make this stylish café a haven of rest. The beautiful ceiling, adorned with restored murals, is worth the visit alone.

Caffè Dante ○ *Dukelských hrdinů.* Open 8am to 11pm Monday to Friday, 11am to 11pm weekends. Lively atmosphere and excellent Italian food make this a popular lunch spot. The cappuccino is the best around. Good for breakfast.

Evropa ○ *Václavské náměstí 25.* Open 7am to midnight. Coffee and liqueurs served in an interesting Art Nouveau interior. The summer terrace is the "in" place to be on a warm summer evening.

The Globe ○ *Janovského 14.* Open 10am to midnight daily. Lively coffeehouse and bar serving meals and alcoholic drinks inside a bookshop specializing in English-language titles.

Kavárna Archa ○ *Na Poříčí 26, Prague 1.* Open 10 am to 11pm weekdays, 11am to 9pm Saturdays, 1pm to 9pm Sundays. Part of a theatre complex, this café is often full of actors.

Kavárna U Anežské ✪ *Anežská 12; Prague 1*. Open daily except Monday 10am to 10pm. Part of a museum complex in the Old Town. St. Agnes Convent houses some fine paintings, so it's possible to combine art and lunch. Lovely garden area. Try the "monk's pocket" for a typical, filling Czech meal.

Paris-Praha ✪-✪✪ *Jindřišská*. Open 9am to 7pm. Not far from Wenceslas Square, this French delicatessen also has a small café (*kavárna*) at the back which serves morning coffee and pastries. Next door, a chic café (also part of the complex) sells coffee and alcoholic drinks until 9pm.

Plha Café ✪ *Corner of Klimenstká and Revoluční*. Open 9am to 10pm. A soothing café-gallery which offers a good selection of coffees and teas in the midst of art exhibits. A bonus for non-smokers — tobacco is banned.

Rock Café ✪ *Národní 20*. By night this pleasant and uncrowded café functions as a busy rock club. A staircase leads down to the café below.

Velryba ✪ *Opatovická 24, Prague 1*. Open daily 11am to 2am. Good selection of drinks and food, with a trendy, Bohemian atmosphere.

U Knihomola ✪ *Mánesova 79, Prague 2*. Downstairs from one of the best-stocked English-language bookstores in Prague, this café has light meals and a lively atmosphere. Open 9am to midnight.

U Zeleného Čaje ✪ *Nerudova 19; Tel 53 26 83*. Open 10am to 7pm. The interior of this café was one of the locations for the shooting of Miloš Forman's film *Amadeus*. The name means "At the Green Tea," and this aromatic tearoom-cum-gift shop serves several different varieties of tea, coffee, and pastries.

ABOUT BERLITZ

In 1878 Professor Maximilian Berlitz had a revolutionary idea about making language learning accessible and enjoyable. One hundred and twenty years later these same principles are still successfully at work.

For language instruction, translation and interpretation services, cross-cultural training, study abroad programs, and an array of publishing products and additional services, visit any one of our more than 350 Berlitz Centers in over 40 countries.

Please consult your local telephone directory for the Berlitz Center nearest you or visit our web site at http://www.berlitz.com.

Helping the World Communicate

CONTENTS